SMART MUFFINS

---

83 Recipes
for Heavenly, Healthful Eating

JANE KINDERLEHRER

Illustrations by Claude Martinot

NEWMARKET PRESS

New York

Quantity Purchases

Companies, professional groups, clubs and other organizations may qualify for special terms when ordering quantities of this title. For information contact: Special Sales Dept., Newmarket Press, 18 East 48th Street, New York, New York 10017, or call (212) 832-3575.

Book design by Ruth Kolbert

Manufactured in the United States of America

First Edition

Dedicated to my favorite muffin-munchers—
Jodi, Becca, Lisa, Hannah, Aaron, Eliana,
Sammy, Tova, Janie, Noah, their parents,
and their Pop-Pop

Also by Jane Kinderlehrer

CONFESSIONS OF A SNEAKY ORGANIC COOK
HOW TO FEEL YOUNGER LONGER
THE ART OF COOKING WITH LOVE AND WHEAT GERM
COOKING KOSHER THE NATURAL WAY
SMART COOKIES

Contents

Introduction 1

What Goes into a Smart Muffin? 5

Making Magnificent Muffins 21

1. Hearty Breakfast Muffins 27

2. Scrumptious Brunch Muffins 41

3. Eat-Your-Vegetables Muffins 51

4. Meals-in-a-Muffin 67

5. Go-Anywhere Fruit 'n' Nut Muffins 87

6. Very Skinny Smart Muffins 103

7. Bless-Your-Heart Muffins 113

8. Life-of-the-Party Muffins 121

9. Smart Muffins for the Allergic 131

10. Exotic Muffins 147

11. Smart Toppings for Smart Muffins 157

Index 163

METRIC CONVERSION CHART

1 teaspoon = 5 ml.   1 tablespoon = 15 ml.
1 ounce = 30 ml.   1 cup = 240 ml./.24 l.
1 quart = 950 ml./.95 l. 1 gallon = 3.80 l.

1 ounce = 28 gr.   1 pound = 454 gr./.454 kg.

F.° 200 225 250 275 300 325 350 375 400 425 450
C.° 93 107 121 135 149 163 177 191 204 218 232

INTRODUCTION

My love for muffins goes back to my early childhood. Mom baked muffins that reflected her mood and our economic status. She made them with extra raisins when she was very pleased with us, like when we got good report cards or practiced the piano without being told. She threw in extra nuts when Dad's business was booming. Streusel toppings appeared on them when company came. She even made muffins when she was troubled about something she had no control over, like the time my brother was in the hospital with a broken leg. They seemed to pick up her spirits—and my brother's.

I even named my favorite doll "Muffin."

There's something very lovable about muffins. They announce their presence with an enticing aroma, bring smiles to cranky sleepy-heads, recharge your body's batteries, and leave you with a sparkle in your eyes and a wonderful taste in your mouth. They're a cinch to make, too, and don't make a big dent in your grocery bill.

Muffins are certainly a delightful way to start the day, but they're not just for breakfast. Their many merits have won them top status as a convenience food that goes to school for lunch, to the office for coffee breaks, into backpacks for nourishment on the trail, and into your handbag for morale-boosting sustenance on the bus, train, or plane. Best of all, they provide a delicious solution to that perpetual question, "What's to eat, Mom?"

But if you, like me, have an urge to see the glow of health on the faces of your loved ones, you will make all your muffins Smart Muffins.

Smart Muffins, like Smart Cookies, do not expand your waistline with empty calories. They don't clog your arteries with lots of fat. Smart Muffins are high in fiber; ridiculously low in fat; and contain no sugar, salt, white flour, hydrogenated fats, or chemical additives. They're rich in nutrients that strengthen bones, like calcium, magnesium, and zinc; nutrients that help you handle stress, like pantothenic acid, a B vitamin that is lost in the refining process; nutrients that contribute to a pleasant disposition like B_1, called the "morale vitamin"; and nutrients that increase vitality, growth, and stamina, like zinc and vitamin E.

California psychiatrist Michael Lesser, in his address before the U.S. Senate Select Committee on Nutrition and Human Needs, quoted the great twelfth-century physician Moses Maimonides:

"No illness which can be treated by diet should be treated by any other means."

I'm not suggesting that you should treat your illnesses with Smart Muffins. I am suggesting that Smart Muffins in your daily diet provide you with many nutrients that can prevent illness. And as everybody knows, an ounce of prevention is worth a pound of cure.

I wrote my previous book, *Smart Cookies,* to make snacking contribute to health instead of to cavities and coronaries. I am delighted to report that it has helped many people get a toehold on the good-nutrition ladder. I get letters from all over the country saying things like, "I never dreamed it was so easy to make nutritious confections." "My kids no longer beg for the store-bought, sugary kind." "My husband loves the Bless-Your-Heart Cookies, and they're so easy to make."

And some said, "I wish you'd do more books on smart cooking. How about one on muffins?"

A challenge like that I can't resist.

Just because these muffins are smart doesn't mean they're boring. I've made them in an infinite variety of ways, for an infinite number of occasions, and for every stage of life—from high chair to rocking chair.

Bridge club at your house tonight? Serve low-calorie Peachy Pecan Muffins. Fantastic—and not a drop of fat or concentrated sweetener. Kids passing up the vegetables? Make Carrot Orange Pecan Muffins or Zucchini Raisin and Nut Muffins, or Orange Parsnip Snowballs. Vegetables never tasted so good!

Smart Muffins are full of tasty surprises—seeds, fruits, honey, raisins, whole grains, vegetables, spices, and a number of other delectable ingredients. These nutritious loaves can be a source of pure joy—not to mention a lifesaver! An assortment of Smart Muffins tucked away in the freezer is better than money in the bank. Let the neighbors drop in. Let the kids bring their hungry friends home. Let the swimmers, the joggers, the marathoners and triathloners barge in ready to eat anything that doesn't move. You'll be ready!

Smart Muffins are, of course, all natural. But according to one of my grandchildren, they have powers that supersede the natural.

Explaining to a friend one day what happens when you depart this world, she said, "God takes you up to Heaven, feeds you my grandma's muffins to make you healthy, then sends you back home."

WHAT GOES INTO
A SMART MUFFIN?

SWEETENERS

Most store-bought muffins—and, indeed, most recipes for muffins—call for sugar as the sweetener. Not Smart Muffins. Sugar provides no body-building protein, no minerals, no vitamins—only empty calories. Yet sugar *needs* vitamin B, especially B_1 or thiamine, to be metabolized. Since it has none of its own, it borrows yours and never pays it back, causing a deficiency in thiamine that can lead to fatigue, neuritis (pains in the joints), and depression.

People always ask me, "But don't we need sugar for energy?" Actually, no! The net effect of eating sugar is in fact a drop in energy, not a gain. Sugar makes a mad rush for your bloodstream, and it raises blood sugar without waiting to make a courtesy call on your liver, which would dole it out slowly. Once in your bloodstream, it raises blood sugar levels to a dangerous high, triggering an outpouring of the hormone insulin. Insulin, in turn, collects sugar from the blood and deposits it in the cells of the body, where it is stored as fat. But the insulin goes in for overkill. It takes practically *all* the sugar out of your blood, leaving you in a dark blue funk, feeling more tired and depressed than before.

Sugar also stimulates other hormones like adrenaline and cortisone, which cause an unhealthy accumulation of triglycerides and cholesterol in the blood. According to Richard A. Kunin, M.D., author of *Mega-Nutrition* (McGraw-Hill, 1980), "The increase in triglycerides thickens the blood, and causes cells to clump, interfering with oxygen transport."

British physician John Yudkin, M.D., says in his book *Sweet and Dangerous* (P. H. Wyden, 1972), "Avoid sugar and you will lessen your chances of getting diabetes, dental decay, atherosclerosis, some forms of cancer, obesity, and gout. You will increase your life span and your chances of enjoying a healthy old age."

To help you live well and live longer, Smart Muffins contain no sugar. Nor do they call for corn syrup, another empty-calorie sweetener. In fact, all sweetening agents have been reduced to a minimum because no concentrated sweetener should be used excessively. Your taste buds will gradually be able to detect and appreciate the natural sweetness present in wholesome foods.

The following sweeteners used in Smart Muffins provide vitamins, minerals, and enzymes—which means they do not deplete your body's supplies and do not make a mad rush to your bloodstream.

Frozen Fruit Juice Concentrates

Fruit juice concentrates are incredibly sweet and rich in nutrients and can be substituted for or used in conjunction with other sweeteners. The fruits they are derived from may vary in sweetness, so give your batter the taste test. You may need a little more of another sweetener for the most appealing flavor.

Honey

Honey is twice as sweet as sugar, so you can use half as much to achieve the same level of sweetness. Honey has other advantages over sugar. Honey's sweetness is derived mainly from fructose, which, unlike sucrose, does not trigger an outpouring of insulin. Fructose is also absorbed into the bloodstream at a much slower rate. It is, therefore, less likely to cause the "sugar blues."

Nutritionally, honey provides B vitamins and small amounts of important minerals like calcium, phosphorus, iron, and potassium, as well as certain enzymes. By contrast, sugar contains no nutrients whatsoever.

Honey should be used raw, unfiltered, and unprocessed. For the least processed honey, you'd have to visit the keeper of the bees! Next best, and more practical, is your health food store. If the honey in your jar has crystallized, rejoice! That's a sign that it has not been damaged by excessive heat. Just put the jar in warm water for a few minutes and the honey will liquefy.

Clover honey is the mildest in flavor and is recommended for baked goods while you are weaning the family away from sugar. Once they are accustomed to the taste of honey, try other varieties. Buckwheat, my favorite, tastes great in muffins if you want the flavor of honey to dominate.

When converting old recipes that call for sugar, use ½ cup honey for every cup of sugar. Reduce the liquid in the recipe by ½ cup for every cup of honey and bake at a temperature 25° F lower than the instructions call for. If there is no liquid in the recipe, add ¼ cup more flour. (There is no need to make these adjustments for the recipes in this book.)

Maple Syrup

Maple syrup contains 65 percent sucrose, as compared to sugar cane and turbinado sugar, both of which are almost 100 percent sucrose. Brown sugar is about 96 percent sucrose. Sucrose is the culprit that triggers the fluctuations in the blood sugar levels mentioned earlier that result in depression and exhaustion.

Look for pure, 100 percent maple syrup. Avoid the maple-flavored syrups, which may contain as little as 2 percent maple syrup and that are in reality 95 percent sucrose.

Molasses

Buy the unsulphured kind. The lighter grades of molasses are sweeter but not quite so nutritious as blackstrap, the third extraction and very rich in minerals. One teaspoon of blackstrap molasses provides 137 milligrams of calcium (as much as you get in ½ glass of milk), 585 milligrams of potassium (more than you get in 2 oranges), and 3.2 milligrams of iron (10 times as much as you get in a tablespoon of raisins), all for only 43 calories. You also get for those same 43 calories an extra bonus of magnesium, zinc, copper, chromium, and small amounts of thiamine, riboflavin, and niacin.

Blackstrap has a strong flavor and only half the sweetening power of sugar. I sometimes use honey or some other sweetener along with blackstrap to temper the flavor.

FLOURS, GRAINS, AND SEEDS

Whole Wheat Flour

Because Smart Muffins call for smart ingredients, we avoid white flour, since it has been emasculated in the refining process. Instead, we use whole wheat flour almost exclusively. The muffins for the allergic call for other types of whole grain flours.

Regular whole wheat flour used in breadmaking is ground from hard winter wheat and contains a high degree of gluten. Gluten gives the flour the ability to absorb more liquid, which helps the dough to rise. Whole wheat pastry flour, the kind recommended for Smart Muffins, contributes to a finer texture. Both kinds contain many life-enhancing nutrients.

Wheat Germ

Unless you are using whole wheat flour, the wheat germ has been removed from most commercial baked goods—breads, cakes, crackers, noodles, cookies, and muffins. Why? Because wheat germ supports life; it attracts life-seeking insects and spoils more readily. Without the wheat germ, flour has a longer shelf life and can be shipped all over the world. It is, therefore, commercially expedient to remove the wheat germ from the flour.

In the "enrichment" process, only 4 of the 33 nutrients contained in wheat germ are actually added to the white flour, and these in only one third the original amount. They are also in a synthetic form, which the body does not use as effectively. The iron that is added, for instance, is inorganic, and interferes with the body's use of vitamin E.

Even though there is some wheat germ in whole wheat flour, I usually add more to Smart Muffins because it contributes a veritable bonanza of nutrients: protein to build and repair cells; polyunsaturated oil for a glowing complexion and efficient metabolism; vitamin E to protect polyunsaturates from oxidation, thus retarding the aging process and damage to the circulatory system; and practically every member of the B-complex family in generous amounts. These vitamins are crucial to maintaining a healthy heart, a positive attitude, and a clear-thinking mind. Some studies have shown that B vitamins can improve the developing intelligence of young children.

Wheat germ also provides a gold mine of minerals: potassium, magnesium, and calcium—all essential to the health of the heart—and zinc, so important to growth in children, to one's senses of taste and smell, to the ability to heal, to a blemish-free complexion, and to the health of the prostate gland.

Wheat germ can be used either raw or toasted. Raw wheat germ has slightly more nutritional value, but it must be very fresh. Toasted wheat germ has better keeping qualities and a flavor more acceptable to some palates.

Keep wheat germ in the refrigerator or in the freezer. It can be used directly from the freezer and will stay fresh longer if kept frozen. Never use rancid wheat germ. If you have a jar that's been around for more than a month, give it a sniff-and-taste test. If it has an off odor or leaves a bitter aftertaste, discard it and get a fresh supply.

Soy Flour

Soy flour is a great protein booster. It has twice as much protein as wheat flour and lots more potassium, calcium, iron, and B-complex vitamins. It also provides lecithin, a substance that helps to emulsify cholesterol.

The amino acids of soy complement those of wheat. (Soy is high in lysine, low in methionine. Wheat is just the opposite.) Together they provide all the essential amino acids in proportions that are most efficiently utilized by the body.

It takes only 2 tablespoons of soy flour at the bottom of a cup of wheat flour to enchance greatly the protein, mineral, and vitamin values of your Smart Muffins.

Rice Flour

Rice flour is made from brown rice and is a good source of iron, protein, minerals, and the B vitamins. Because it is so low in sodium, it is frequently recommended for salt-free diets. It can be used measure for measure as a substitute for wheat flour for those allergic to wheat.

Rice polish, also known as rice bran, is ground from the outer coating of the rice grain. It is an excellent source of the B vitamin niacin, which has been shown to lower cholesterol levels. It is a good source of fiber, too.

Popcorn Flour

Popcorn flour is not available commercially. You make it yourself from freshly popped corn, with no fat or salt added. It takes about 1¼ cups of popped corn to make 1 cup of flour. Grind the popped corn in a blender or seed mill. It contributes a pleasant, corny flavor to your Smart Muffins. Its most attractive asset is its low calorie content—only 50 calories in a cup, as compared to 400 calories in a cup of wheat flour. It is so light and airy, however, that it cannot be used without the support of heavier flours.

Oats

Oat is one grain that somehow managed to survive the refining process with most of its nutrients intact. Rolled oats is simply the generic name for ordinary, commercially available cereal oats or oatmeal. I prefer the nutty flavor of the old-fashioned kind over the instant. Oats are a good source of B vitamins, calcium, potassium, and protein, and contain very little sodium. A little more than 1 cup of oats whizzed in blender or seed mill will give you a cup of oat flour.

Cornmeal

Commercially available cornmeal has been stripped of many nutrients as well as the amino acids tryptophan and lysine. Look for stone-ground or water-ground cornmeal. They have undergone much less processing. Their nutritional value and flavor are far superior. Bolted cornmeal has undergone only a rather crude sifting to remove hulls, a process that slightly lowers fiber and calcium content but does not affect other nutrients.

My first choice is Hi-Lysine cornmeal derived from a recently developed breed of corn containing high levels of amino acids, especially tryptophan and lysine. Besides providing the necessary amino acids in the proportions in which the body uses them, Hi-Lysine cornmeal is organically grown and ground from the whole kernel, including the hull for extra fiber. It is now available at many health-food stores, or you can order it from E and D Grain Co., Fullerton, Nebraska 68638.

Millet Flour

Millet flour is ground from millet seed, a grain so rich in minerals that, unlike other grains, it is alkaline-forming rather than acid-forming, making it a perfect addition to the diets of ulcer and colitis patients. Millet is high in protein and B vitamins and is, in fact, the most nutritious of the grain family—and the most neglected. It is a major food source for the long-lived Hunza people of the Himalayas and the taller, stronger natives of northern China. Yet in the United States it has been dubbed "the poor man's cereal" and is mainly used and considered for the birds.

Wheat Bran

Bran is the outer coating of the wheat berry, which is removed in the refining process. Bran is a good source of B vitamins and minerals and an excellent source of fiber. Stripped from the wheat, bran is an aid to the digestive system and has been shown to provide protection against polyps and diseases of the colon. It also protects against gall bladder disease and it decreases the absorption of cholesterol and unfriendly fats, significantly reducing the incidence of cardiovascular disease.

Bran absorbs eight times its volume in water. Be sure to increase your liquid intake when you add bran to your diet.

Like wheat germ, bran should be refrigerated or kept in the freezer. It can be used directly from the freezer.

Oat Bran

Oat bran, the new wonder kid on the cereal block, has been shown to help stabilize blood sugar in diabetes and hypoglycemia. More than any other cereal, oat bran will help to reduce fats and cholesterol in the body. It is rich in water-soluble fiber, the kind that slows the absorption of carbohydrates. Because of the high-density lipoprotein found in oats, oat bran provides a measure of protection against arteriosclerosis. Oat bran concentrates the protein, minerals, and vitamins found in oats and is very low in sodium.

Seeds

When you stop to think about it, the seed is the very core of life. Its tiny kernal contains a mysterious and fantastic concentration of energy and nutrients designed by Nature, the master chemist, to get the plant up and keep it growing. This core of life in seeds brings vitality to those who consume them.

Consider the powerhouse of nutrients you get in seeds. They are a remarkable, unspoiled source of unsaturated fatty acids. Sunflower seeds are especially high in precious linoleic acid, which helps to prevent harmful deposits of cholesterol and improves resistance to disease by strengthening connective tissue in the cells.

All seeds are rich in nutrients. Pumpkin seeds are 30 percent protein, and high in iron, calcium, phosphorus, and zinc. Sesame seeds are 45 percent protein, and rich in polyunsaturates that are so good for the heart and blood vessels.

Seeds are also rich in vitamin E, which helps maintain normal viscosity in the blood, thus lessening the risk of life-threatening blood clots. They also contain high amounts of the B vitamins—more than you get, in fact, in an equivalent quantity of wheat germ. They are an excellent source of minerals, as well, including the important trace minerals.

One of the most valuable contributions of seeds is their store of enzymes, which initiate and fulfill all vital processes in the cells. Enzymes are as fragile as they are vital, and cooking destroys many of them. Therefore, many of the recipes in *Smart Muffins* call for seeds as a garnish, unexposed to heat, so you can reap full value from their life-enhancing nutrients.

A seed mill is a very useful piece of equipment for grinding seeds into meal. It can also be used to grind nuts and pulverize dried orange and lemon peel into powdered rind. It handles small quantities very efficiently. You'll find them at specialty shops and in some health-food stores. A coffee grinder can be used instead, if you prefer.

FATS

Polyunsaturates

Safflower, sunflower, soy, and corn oil are polyunsaturated oils providing essential fatty acids, important building blocks for every cell in the body. They are called essential because the body cannot manufacture them—they must be consumed. Polyunsaturates have another function: They lower the LDL (low-density lipoprotein) content of cholesterol, a maneuver that contributes to cardiovascular health. LDL's are the bad guys in the cholesterol family. They contribute to the formation of artery-clogging clots. However, polyunsaturates also tend to lower HDL (high-density lipoproteins), which tend to protect the arteries by preventing formation of clots.

Polyunsaturates are also chemically very reactive, meaning they are converted by oxygen into peroxides, which break down into free radicals that damage the cells of the body, causing a predisposition to aging and malignancies. Nature, in her infinite wisdom, packages these fatty acids with vitamin E, an antioxidant. It prevents peroxidation, but processing removes the vitamin E. It is therefore important to supplement your intake of polyunsaturated oils with vitamin E, both internally and externally—that is, besides the vitamin E you take as a supplement, protect the oils in your salad dressing by squeezing the contents of a 400 I.U. vitamin E capsule in each pint of polyunsaturated oil.

Mono-Unsaturates

Olive oil and peanut oil are mono-unsaturates. Sesame oil is very close to being a mono-unsaturate.

One of the most exciting developments in nutrition is our new understanding of the role of dietary fats in the pursuit and maintenance of health. For some time it was thought that mono-unsaturates were neutral, that they neither lowered nor raised cholesterol levels. But a study by Fred Mattson, Ph.D., of the University of California at San Diego, reveals that mono-unsaturates are *cholesterol reducers* just as effective as the polyunsaturates. But whereas both types of fat reduce the LDL fraction, the mono-unsaturates do not (as the polyunsaturates do) lower the HDL, and in some instances the mono-unsaturates actually raise the HDL. The ability of the mono-unsaturates to lower the bad fraction and increase the good fraction makes them an even better friend of the cardiovascular system than the polyunsaturates.

Also, the mono-unsaturates are more stable than the polyunsaturates, less subject to peroxidation or rancidity, and more stable when exposed to heat. For this reason, the mono-unsaturates are preferable for cooking and baking.

Butter

Pure, unsalted butter is the kind that goes into Smart Muffins in those recipes that call for butter, but the amount is greatly reduced from most muffin recipes. In small amounts, butter is a perfectly good food that has been used and enjoyed for countless generations.

Do *not* substitute margarine for butter. Healthwise, you're much better off with butter. The process of hydrogenation converts the polyunsaturates that go into margarine into a form that is even more damaging to the arteries than saturated fats or cholesterol. The American Heart Association and the National Cancer Institute both recommend a diet containing no more than 30 percent of calories from fat, with equal amounts from all three types: 10 percent polyunsaturates, 10 percent mono-unsaturates, and 10 percent saturated fat. Leave some room in your saturated fat allotment for the pleasure of butter.

OTHER INGREDIENTS

Carob

Carob powder is derived from the fruit of the carob tree. The carob pods are dried, seeded, and skinned. In ancient times, the seed of the carob pod was used as the standard for the weight of the carat, still used as the standard for the measurement of precious metals and jewels. Carob is also known as St. John's bread. Legend has it that St. John survived on the fruit of the carob tree while he was in the desert. It is also known in yiddish as *boeksur* (pronounced "boxer") and is distributed to Jewish children on the holiday Tu B'Shevat, which celebrates the life-giving quality of the carob tree.

Because it is a life-giving substance, carob is used in Smart Muffins to replace chocolate. The taste and color are quite similar. Unlike chocolate, however, carob has no theobromine (a caffeinelike substance); no oxalic acid, which binds with calcium and sometimes causes kidney stones; no fat; and very few calories. And, unlike chocolate, carob contains natural sweeteners and therefore requires fewer added sweeteners. Its carbohydrates are derived from fruit sugars, which have a low fat content: 2 percent in carob compared to 52 percent in chocolate. The pectin content of carob has proved valuable in the treatment of diarrhea.

If your family is unaccustomed to the slightly different taste and aroma of carob, adding a tablespoon or two of cocoa to the carob container will make the whole thing taste like cocoa.

Lecithin

Lecithin is another marvelous, life-enhancing substance that is used in Smart Muffins. Recent research done in Israel revealed that as little as 1 tablespoon of lecithin granules daily was able to lower LDL cholesterol levels and triglycerides significantly. It also reduced plaque formation in the bloodstream. That alone should be enough to make you reach for the lecithin granules, but there's more. Lecithin can keep you on your toes mentally. M.I.T. scientists have shown that lecithin in the diet improves memory and actually makes one "smarter." It does this by helping the body to manufacture acetyl-choline, a substance that helps the brain to transmit nerve signals. Soybeans and eggs are both good sources of lecithin.

Grated Orange Rind

Many of the recipes in *Smart Muffins* call for grated orange rind, not only for its flavor, but also for its many important nutrients—vitamin C, vitamin A, calcium, trace minerals, and the important bioflavenoids which strengthen cartilage, preventing varicose veins, bleeding gums, and a host of other ailments.

Here's how to have an endless supply: Every time you use an orange, wash it thoroughly with a stiff brush, then dry it. Using a vegetable peeler, peel off the orange layer of skin. Wrap this skin in paper toweling and place it in a warm place to dry. When it is dry and brittle, store it in a jar. When a recipe calls for orange rind, put a handful of these dried rinds in your seed mill, coffee grinder, or blender. You'll have lovely fresh-ground orange rind with an enticing aroma and flavor.

Baking Powder

Look for a brand of baking powder that is aluminum-free. Royal Baking Powder is a good commercial brand without aluminum. Cellu, another brand available at most health-food stores, is both aluminum- and sodium-free.

You can make your own baking powder by combining ¼ teaspoon of baking soda with ½ teaspoon of cream of tartar. This is equivalent to 1 teaspoon of baking powder. To make a larger supply, combine 1 tablespoon of baking soda, 2 tablespoons of cream of tartar, and 2 tablespoons of arrowroot powder. The arrowroot protects the other two ingredients from absorbing moisture and reacting on each other. Seal tightly and store in a cool, dry place. Makes ¼ cup.

Sour Milk

Sour milk may be used as a substitute for buttermilk or yogurt in Smart Muffins. To make sour milk, simply add 2 teaspoons of lemon juice or vinegar to a cup of milk.

MAKING
MAGNIFICENT
MUFFINS

Muffins are a joy to eat and, because they're so quick and easy, a joy to make! Here are some guidelines.

Muffin batter can be mixed by hand, mixing machine, or in a food processor. If you make them by hand, combine all the dry ingredients in one bowl, the wet ingredients in another. Make a well in the middle of the dry ingredients. Add the wet ingredients and, with a few broad strokes of a wide spatula, mix together only until the ingredients are well combined. The batter should be a little lumpy and should drop from the spoon cleanly in blobs.

Beware of overmixing. Besides causing humps, cracks, and tunnels, overmixing develops the gluten in the flour, which is fine for yeast-risen breads but not for muffins. Gluten makes for a tough-textured muffin. Mix with as few strokes as possible only until all the flour is moistened and no dry white areas of flour are visible. Add raisins, chopped dates, seeds, or nuts to the batter during the last few strokes to avoid damaging them in the mixing process.

Undermixing, on the other hand, makes for a flat-top muffin of low volume, with lumps of dry flour and a crumbly texture.

A muffin that has been mixed just enough will have a rounded top, straight sides, and an even-textured crumb, and no tunnels.

Using a Food Processor

If you are using a food processor, combine the wet ingredients in the processor bowl, and process to combine. Then add the combined dry ingredients and mix wet and dry together with 5 or 6 pushes on the processor pulse button or until no flour is visible.

Before Baking

To rise to perfection, muffins need a hot oven—about 400 degrees. Have the oven preheated to the baking temperature and muffins pans prepared before combining the wet and dry ingredients. As soon as the two mixtures are combined, hustle the batter into the prepared muffin pans and into the oven to take full advantage of the rising power of the leavening agents. Fill the cups ⅔ full and place the muffin tins in the upper half of the oven. A soup ladle makes even distribution of the batter easy. If there isn't enough batter to fill all the cups, add water to the empty ones. This makes for even heat distribution and prevents scorching of the tins.

For oversize muffins—the ones that seem to be wearing cowboy hats—fill the muffin tins almost to the top, but grease the top of the tins to prevent sticking.

Use heavyweight muffin tins for burn-resistant, fluffy results. If heavyweight muffin tins are not available, use 2 muffin tins of the same size, set inside each other.

Muffin tins can be greased with oil or butter or a mixture of liquid lecithin and oil. To have a convenient supply of this mixture on hand, mix together in a small container ¼ cup of oil and ¼ cup of liquid lecithin. Shake it up and refrigerate. It becomes semisolid and is a very convenient blend for quickly greasing your muffin tins. If you prefer, you can use paper or foil liners and you will not need to grease or wash the tins.

Plumping Raisins and Toasting Nuts

To plump raisins or any dried fruit, put the fruit in a steamer basket over about ½ cup of water. Cover and steam for about 5 minutes. Or: Pour boiling water to cover over dried fruit in a small bowl. Let soak until plumped, about a half hour. Drain well and pat dry.

To toast sunflower seeds or nuts, spread in a single layer on a baking sheet and toast the seeds or nuts in a 350-degree oven for about 5 minutes for seeds, 7 to 10 minutes for nuts. Shake the pan once or twice and watch them closely (they burn easily). Nuts and seeds can also be toasted in a skillet on top of the stove, using moderate heat.

Baking, Cooling, and Storing

Most regular-size muffins are done in 20 to 25 minutes, miniatures in 12 to 15 minutes. Muffins are done when a cake tester or wooden pick inserted into the center comes out clean.

Allow muffins to cool for about 5 minutes before removing them from the muffin tins; then place them on a wire rack. Allow them to cool completely before storing in refrigerator or freezer. You'll find that paper baking cups can be removed much more easily when the muffins are cool.

You can fill the house with the wonderful aroma of muffins in the oven even on hectic mornings. Simply freeze muffin batter in foil baking cups. When frozen solid, keep them in plastic bags for easier storage. Mark each package with pertinent data—like the name of the muffin, the type of flour it's made from (for the benefit of those who have allergies to certain types), whether or not it contains dairy products, and the baking temperature. Allow 10 minutes' extra time for baking.

You can also store muffin batter in the refrigerator and bake only what you need for each day's enjoyment. The batter will keep for about five days. Keep in mind, though, that the longer the batter is kept, the lower the volume of the baked muffin.

There are times when you will want to reheat muffins that have already been baked. There are several ways to keep muffins from drying out when reheating. You can cut them in halves, sprinkle each half with a few drops of water or fruit juice, then warm in a toaster oven. Or you can warm them in a steamer. You can also store baked muffins in the freezer, each one wrapped individually in foil. When reheating, place them in the oven in their foil wrappers. If, through oversight, muffins become overly dry, all is not lost. Crumble them up and use the crumbs as the base of a delicious trifle. Top the crumbs with yogurt, fruit, and nuts.

Smart Muffins Are Different

Smart Muffins are not as sweet as those your family may be accustomed to eating. Until their taste buds are educated to detect the sweetness in natural foods, serve the muffins with a conserve that adds sweetness without added sweeteners. You can make these yourself by cooking fruit in fruit juice to the consistency of apple butter, or you can buy conserves ready-made in many varieties. I like the Sorrell Ridge brand, but there are others. Read the labels. You'll find them in gourmet shops, health-food stores, and many supermarkets.

1

HEARTY
BREAKFAST MUFFINS

Did you know . . .

- that what you eat for breakfast can affect your energy level at three in the afternoon?
- that according to a recent survey, eating a good breakfast can improve your chances of living longer?
- that eating a good breakfast means less fatigue and less fluid retention?
- that if you are skipping breakfast to lose weight, you are defeating your own purpose? Skipping breakfast keeps your metabolism in low gear. To burn fat and calories, you want to shift into high gear.

Jeffrey S. Bland, Ph.D., director of research projects for the Linus Pauling Institute of Science and author of several books, including *Your Health Under Siege: Using Nutrition to Fight Back* (Stephen Greene Press, 1981), says the ideal breakfast should be rich in complex carbohydrates and protein and contain a little fat.

Hearty Breakfast Muffins fulfill those requirements in a most delicious way. Not only do they provide complex carbohydrates for high-level energy, they also have lots of fiber for protection against polyps and cancer of the colon; seeds and nuts for important minerals, and polyunsaturated fats that keep your skin soft and lovely; whole grains with B vitamins that can actually lighten your mood, help fight stress, and sustain your energy; and spices that enhance flavors and fill the house with enticing aromas.

If you are too rushed to eat a good breakfast, slip some of these muffins into your briefcase and into the childen's schoolbags. You'll find they have excellent satiety value. You won't be distracted by hunger pangs long before lunch.

Wheat Germ Raisin Ginger Muffins

Your body never had it so good! Oat bran tends to lower cholesterol. Wheat bran provides fiber, so essential to the health of your colon. Wheat germ provides vitamins that can actually improve your disposition. (It contains vitamin B_1, known as the "morale vitamin" because it helps you achieve an upbeat attitude.) It also provides pantothenic acid—known as the "antistress vitamin"—which helps you to cope with the exigencies of the morning rush hour. The spices provide a festival for your taste buds.

½ cup wheat bran
1 cup buttermilk or yogurt
2 large eggs
2 tablespoons olive oil
3 tablespoons molasses or
    honey
½ cup apple sauce
1 cup sifted whole wheat
    pastry flour
¼ cup wheat germ

¼ cup oat bran
1 teaspoon baking powder
1 teaspoon baking soda
½ teaspoon ground ginger
½ teaspoon cinnamon
⅛ teaspoon ground cloves
1 teaspoon grated orange rind
½ cup plumped raisins
½ cup toasted sunflower seeds

In a small bowl, combine the bran and buttermilk or yogurt, and mix well. Set aside.

In another bowl or food processor, combine the eggs, olive oil, molasses or honey, and the applesauce. Process to combine, then add the bran mixture and process again.

Combine the flour, wheat germ, oat bran, baking powder, baking soda, and spices, and add this mixture to the wet ingredients. Process briefly just until no flour is visible. Stir in the plumped raisins.

Preheat oven to 375°F. Spoon the batter into 12 muffin cups greased with a lecithin and oil mixture. Garnish with sunflower seeds and bake for 15 to 20 minutes.

Yield: 12 muffins.

Approximately 147 calories each.

Dynamite Muffins

These high-fiber fruit-and-nut gems pack a terrific nutritional wallop and provide all the essential amino acids. They're great for breakfast on the run, backpacking, lunch boxes, or as an afternoon pickup.

1 cup orange, pineapple, or apple juice
½ cup bran
3 eggs
3 tablespoons olive oil, vegetable oil, or softened sweet butter
¼ cup molasses
1 cup applesauce
½ cup raisins, plumped
¼ cup apricots, diced
¼ cup prunes, diced
¼ cup soy flour
1½ cups whole wheat flour

½ cup dry milk powder
⅓ cup wheat germ
2 tablespoons lecithin granules
2 tablespoons oat bran
2 teaspoons baking powder
½ teaspoon baking soda
1 teaspoon cinnamon
¼ teaspoon ginger
¼ teaspoon nutmeg
1 tablespoon grated orange rind
½ cup walnuts, chopped
¼ cup peanuts, chopped

In a small bowl, combine the fruit juice and bran. Set aside.

In a large mixing bowl or food processor, mix together the eggs, oil or butter, molasses, and applesauce. Stir in the bran mixture. Add the raisins and chopped fruit.

In another bowl, stir together the flours, milk powder, wheat germ, lecithin granules, oat bran, baking powder, baking soda, spices, and orange rind.

Add the flour mixture to the wet ingredients and mix just enough to moisten the flour. Stir in the nuts.

Preheat oven to 375°F.

Grease 24 regular-size muffin cups or 5 dozen minicups with butter or a mixture of liquid lecithin and oil, or line with paper baking cups. Spoon the batter into the muffin cups. Top each with ½ pecan or ½ walnut or ¼ teaspoon blueberry or strawberry conserve.

Bake 12 minutes in the upper half of the oven for minimuffins, 20 minutes for regular-size muffins, or until lightly browned and dry inside when pierced with a cake tester or wooden pick.

Yield: 2 dozen regular-size muffins or 5 dozen minimuffins.

Approximately 124 calories each for regular-size muffins, approximately 50 calories each for minimuffins.

Wheat Sprout Muffins

You won't believe how wonderfully good-tasting these muffins are, while being loaded with life-enhancing nutrients. Wheat sprouts have an anticancer effect, according to researchers at the University of Texas. (See *Nutrition & Cancer*, Fall 1978.) Sprouting causes an explosion of nutrients, especially the vitamin B's, and increases the development of vitamin C. Teenagers love 'em.

3 eggs, separated	1 cup sunflower seeds
1 tablespoon olive or vegetable oil	½ cup coconut
1 tablespoon molasses	1 tablespoon grated orange rind
1 cup wheat sprouts	½ cup raisins, plumped

In a mixing bowl or food processor, blend together the egg yolks, oil, and molasses. Stir in the sprouts, seeds, coconut, orange rind, and raisins. Fold in the beaten egg whites.

Preheat oven to 400°F. Line 12 regular-size muffin wells with foil baking cups, or grease with a mixture of lecithin and oil.

Spoon the batter into the muffin wells and bake for about 15 to 20 minutes or until nicely browned.

Yield: 12 muffins.

Approximately 150 calories each.

HOW TO GROW WHEAT SPROUTS

Put 4 tablespoons of wheat grains (available at health-food stores and large supermarkets) in a pint jar. Give them a quick rinse to remove surface dirt, then fill the jar ⅔ full with tepid water. Cover and let stand overnight. The next morning, cover the jar with two layers of cheesecloth secured with a rubber band, or with a screened lid available at gourmet and health-food stores. You can make your own from window screen cut to fit a jar ring.

Without removing the screened lid, pour off the soak water, but do not discard it. Use it in soup or in cooking water for vegetables, or to replace the fat in a stir-fry.

Next, rinse the grains with tepid water, pour off the rinse water (give it to your plants), and let the jar rest under the sink or on the sink, slightly tilted so excess moisture can drain off. Use a sponge or folded dishcloth to prop up the jar bottom. Cover the jar with a tea towel if you're keeping it on the sink—the grains germinate best in the dark.

Repeat the rinsing procedure 2 or 3 times throughout the next 2 days. By the end of the second day, your wheat sprouts should be almost as long as the grain and ready for use. Refrigerate them until you're ready to use them.

Follow the same procedure for other grains such as triticale and rye and for garbanzo beans (chick-peas).

Maple Walnut Muffins

The lovely flavor of maple syrup mingled with the crunch of walnuts, which permeates every bite of these muffins, always evokes for me the memory of the corner ice-cream store where maple walnut was my standard order.

2 eggs
3 tablespoons walnut oil or
    unsalted butter, softened
¼ cup maple syrup
½ cup milk
½ cup whole wheat pastry flour

¼ cup wheat germ
¼ cup oat bran
2 teaspoons baking powder
1 teaspoon baking soda
½ cup chopped walnuts

In a bowl or food processor, mix together the eggs, oil or butter, maple syrup, and milk.

In another bowl combine the pastry flour, wheat germ, bran, baking powder, and baking soda. Process briefly, then stir in the nuts.

Preheat oven to 350°F and spoon the batter into 12 muffin cups greased with a lecithin and oil mixture. Bake for 20 to 25 minutes or until toasty brown.

Yield: 12 muffins.

Approximately 127 calories each.

Date and Nut Muffins

There are lots of hardworking nutrients in these fabulous-tasting muffins. The dates contribute a lovely natural sweetness, lots of potassium (so necessary for the smooth functioning of the muscles that control the beat of your heart), and goodly amounts of calcium, iron, phosphorus, niacin, and vitamin A.

1 teaspoon baking soda
1 cup boiling water
½ cup dates, cut in thirds
½ cup raisins
2 eggs
1 teaspoon vanilla
1 tablespoon walnut, olive, or
    vegetable oil
1 tablespoon honey
1 tablespoon molasses

2 tablespoons wheat bran
1¾ cups sifted whole wheat
    pastry flour
3 tablespoons wheat germ
4 tablespoons lecithin granules
2 tablespoons oat bran
1 teaspoon baking powder
1 tablespoon grated orange
    rind
½ cup chopped walnuts

Add the baking soda to the boiling water. Soak the dates and raisins in the water for about 10 minutes or until slightly softened.

In a small bowl or food processor, blend together the eggs, vanilla, oil, honey, and molasses. Add the wheat bran and the date-raisin mixture with the liquid they were soaked in.

In another bowl, mix together the flour, wheat germ, lecithin granules, oat brans, baking powder, and orange rind.

Preheat oven to 400°F. Line 12 regular-size muffin wells with paper or foil liners, or grease with a mixture of lecithin and oil.

Combine the wet and dry ingredients and mix briefly just to moisten the dry ingredients, then stir in the nuts. Spoon into the muffin wells and bake for about 20 minutes or until a cake tester comes out clean.

Yield: 12 large muffins.

Approximately 170 calories each.

Hearty Pear and Pecan Muffins

I haven't the vaguest idea what makes these high-risers peak to perfectly. Our kids call them skyscrapers and light up like the Fourth of July when I have a batch ready for after-school snacking.

2 large eggs
¼ cup maple syrup
2 tablespoons olive, walnut, or vegetable oil
½ cup buttermilk or yogurt
1 teaspoon vanilla
2 tablespoons wheat bran
1½ cups sifted whole wheat pastry flour
2 tablespoons wheat germ
3 tablespoons lecithin granules
2 tablespoons oat bran

1 teaspoon baking powder
1 teaspoon baking soda
1 teaspoon cinnamon
1 tablespoon grated orange rind
⅛ teaspoon grated nutmeg
1½ cups coarsely chopped cored pears
½ cup chopped pecans (walnuts, hazelnuts, or peanuts may be substituted)

In a mixing bowl or food processor, blend together the eggs, maple syrup, oil, buttermilk or yogurt, vanilla, and wheat bran.

In another bowl, mix together the flour, wheat germ, lecithin granules, oat bran, baking powder, baking soda, cinnamon, orange rind, and nutmeg.

Preheat oven to 400°F. Line 12 regular-size muffin cups with baking liners, or grease with a mixture of lecthin and oil.

Combine the wet and dry ingredients and mix briefly, just to moisten the dry ingredients. Stir in the pears and nuts. Spoon the batter into the muffin wells and bake for about 18 minutes or until the muffins are nicely rounded, golden brown, and a cake tester comes out clean.

Yield: 12 muffins.

Approximately 161 calories each.

Fig and Nut Muffins

The fragrance of these muffins will wake up your late-for-breakfast sleepyheads. Figs have exceptional nutritional value and are easy to digest. They provide protein, fiber, vitamins A and B, and the bioflavenoids, which strengthen your cartilage. Serve plain with butter or fancy with cream cheese, cherry preserves, or orange marmalade.

½ cup chopped figs soaked in
    ¼ cup orange juice
1 cup yogurt
½ cup unprocessed bran
2 large eggs
2 tablespoons molasses
1 tablespoon honey
2 tablespoons olive oil or
    softened butter
1½ cups sifted whole wheat
    pastry flour

1¼ cups soy flour
2 tablespoons oat bran
1 teaspoon baking soda
1 teaspoon baking powder
1 teaspoon cinnamon
1 teaspoon grated orange rind
½ cup plumped raisins
½ cup toasted walnuts,
    chopped
walnuts for garnishing

In a small bowl, combine the fig and orange juice mixture with the yogurt and bran. Set aside. In a large bowl or food processor, combine the eggs, molasses, honey, and oil or butter. Process to combine. In another bowl, combine the flours, oat bran, baking soda, baking powder, cinnamon, and orange rind.

Preheat oven to 400°F. Grease 12 muffin cups with a lecithin and oil mixture or line with paper baking cups.

Add the wet to the dry ingredients and process just long enough to combine. Stir in the raisins and nuts.

Spoon the batter into the muffin cups and garnish each muffin with ½ walnut. Bake in the upper half of the oven for about 20 minutes or until golden and a cake tester comes out clean. Allow to cool for 5 minutes, then turn out onto a rack.

Yield: 12 large muffins.

Approximately 176 calories each.

Peanut Butter Banana Muffins

Kids go bananas over these treats. They fluff up like popovers and are great for parties, for breakfast, and for after-school nourishment. Bananas are an excellent source of potassium.

⅔ cup peanut butter
½ cup mashed bananas
¾ cup yogurt or buttermilk
3 tablespoons honey
1 teaspoon vanilla
2 eggs
1¼ cups sifted whole wheat
    pastry flour
¼ cup soy flour

1 teaspoon cinnamon
1 teaspoon baking powder
1 teaspoon baking soda
¼ cup toasted sunflower seeds
4 tablespoons unsweetened
    blackberry or straw-
    berry conserve
peanuts for garnish

Preheat oven to 400°F. Grease 12 muffin cups with a lecithin and oil mixture or line with baking cups.

In a bowl or food processor, mix together the peanut butter, bananas, yogurt or buttermilk, honey, vanilla, and eggs.

In another bowl, combine the flours, cinnamon, baking powder, and baking soda. Process or mix to combine the wet and dry ingredients. Stir in the sunflower seeds.

Half fill the muffin cups, top with a teaspoon of conserve, then top with the remaining batter. Sprinkle with peanuts. Bake in the upper half of the oven for 20 to 25 minutes or until rounded tops are tinged with gold and a cake tester comes out clean.

Yield: 12 muffins.

Approximately 165 calories each.

2
SCRUMPTIOUS
BRUNCH MUFFINS

A brunch is informal, relaxing, chummy, easy on the hostess, and my favorite way to entertain, especially during the hectic holiday season, when the children are home from college, the married ones come home with a "pride" of grandchildren, and everyone wants to visit, get together with old friends and classmates, and catch up on what's new.

These brunch muffins are a little more exotic than the breakfast muffins but no less wholesome. The Peachy Beany Spice Muffins are very rich in fiber, which, by decreasing the absorption of cholesterol and unfriendly fats, significantly reduces the incidence of cardiovascular disease.

The Orange Marmalade Poppy Seed Muffins provide a good supply of zinc, which stimulates immune cell production, thus providing a measure of protection against disease.

The Wheat Sprout Muffins provide vitamin E, which helps maintain normal viscosity in the blood, thus lessening the risk of damaging blood clots.

All of these muffins freeze well, making it possible to make a variety ahead of time and be ready for any sudden invasion. Warm them in the oven to put a toasty crust on them before serving. The enticing aroma will add another dimension to the fun and cordiality.

You could make it a "muffin brunch" and serve them with an assortment of sensational toppings like yogurt cream cheese blended with strawberry conserves, banana-orange jam, or apricot-almond spread.

Peachy Beany Spice Muffins

Beans and grains have complementary amino acids that make these muffins a complete protein source. The beans contribute iron, calcium, magnesium, and fiber, and the peaches make them taste like fruitcake.

1 cup cooked pinto beans,
   mashed
2 tablespoons olive or vegetable
   oil
2 tablespoons honey or
   molasses
1 egg
1 teaspoon vanilla
2 tablespoons yogurt or
   buttermilk
½ cup sifted whole wheat
   pastry flour

2 tablespoons wheat germ
1 teaspoon baking powder
1 teaspoon baking soda
½ teaspoon cinnamon
¼ teaspoon nutmeg
¼ teaspoon ground cloves
1 cup diced peaches (1 large)
½ cup diced prunes
¼ cup chopped nuts

If you're using a food processor, put the beans in the processor bowl with the oil, honey or molasses, egg, and vanilla, and process until the beans are mashed.

If you're using a mixing bowl, mash the beans and blend with the oil, honey or molasses, beaten egg, vanilla, and yogurt or buttermilk.

In another bowl, combine the flour, wheat germ, baking powder, baking soda, and spices.

Preheat oven to 375°F. Stir in the fruit and nuts. Spoon the mixture into foil muffin cups and bake for about 25 minutes or until a cake tester comes out clean.

Yield: 12 muffins.

Approximately 109 calories each.

Orange Marmalade Poppy Seed Muffins

Poppy seeds are a good source of important enzymes, the B vitamins, and many minerals—including zinc, which is essential to healing, to your sense of taste, to healthy bones, and to growth in children.

1 large egg
2 tablespoons frozen orange
    juice concentrate (slightly
    thawed)
2 tablespoons honey or
    molasses
2 tablespoons olive oil or
    softened butter
½ cup yogurt or buttermilk
2 tablespoons wheat bran
⅓ cup unsweetened orange
    marmalade (Sorrell Ridge)
1½ cups sifted whole wheat
    pastry flour

3 tablespoons poppy seeds
2 tablespoons lecithin granules
2 tablespoons wheat germ
2 tablespoons oat bran
1 tablespoon grated orange
    rind
1 teaspoon baking powder
1 teaspoon baking soda
    orange glaze (2 tablespoons
    orange marmalade mixed
    with 1 tablespoon boiling
    water)

In a mixing bowl or food processor, blend together the egg, orange concentrate, honey or molasses, oil or butter, yogurt or buttermilk, bran, and marmalade.

In another bowl, mix together the flour, seeds, lecithin granules, wheat germ, oat bran, orange rind, baking powder, and baking soda.

Preheat oven to 400°F. Line 12 muffin wells with paper baking cups, or grease with a mixture of lecithin and oil.

Combine the wet and dry mixtures and stir only until the dry ingredients are moistened. Spoon the batter into the muffin wells and bake for about 20 minutes or until a cake tester comes out clean. Brush the tops of the muffins with the orange glaze.

Yield: 12 muffins.

Approximately 102 calories each.

Coffee Cake Muffins

Light, fluffy, tender, crusty—fantastic! Enjoy them hot from the oven . . . and in good conscience. The lecithin and oat bran tend to lower both triglycerides and cholesterol.

BATTER

- 1 cup yogurt or sour cream or half of each
- 1 teaspoon baking soda
- ¼ cup sweet butter, softened
- 4 tablespoons honey
- 2 eggs
- 1 teaspoon vanilla

- 2 cups sifted whole wheat pastry flour
- 2 tablespoons lecithin granules
- 2 tablespoons wheat germ
- 2 tablespoons oat bran
- 2 teaspoons baking powder

TOPPING

- ½ cup unsweetened ground coconut
- ½ cup chopped nuts

- 1 teaspoon cinnamon
- 1 teaspoon grated orange rind

Stir the baking soda into the sour cream or yogurt and set aside.

In a mixing bowl or a food processor, blend together the butter, honey, eggs, and vanilla. Stir in the sour cream mixture.

In another bowl, mix together the pastry flour, lecithin granules, wheat germ, oat bran, and baking powder.

Preheat oven to 350°F. Grease 12 regular-size muffin cups with a lecithin and oil mixture or with butter.

Combine the topping ingredients. Put 2 tablespoons of batter in each muffin cup. Divide the topping mixture in half. Distribute half over the batter. Add the rest of the muffin batter, then top each with the rest of the topping mixture. Bake for 20 to 25 minutes.

Yield: 12 muffins.

Approximately 200 calories each.

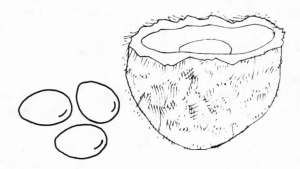

Herbed Minibiscuit Muffins

A savory bell-ringer for parties or a wonderful accompaniment for the tray of crudités. The buttermilk provides an acid environment that helps the body assimilate calcium, iron, magnesium, and zinc.

1⅔ cups whole wheat pastry flour
2 tablespoons wheat bran
2 tablespoons wheat germ
2 tablespoons oat bran
2 teaspoons baking powder
½ teaspoon baking soda
3 tablespoons mixed fresh herbs, or use basil, marjoram, chives, dill, and sage—or a mixture of any of these

3 teaspoons dried herbs
¼ cup sweet butter
⅔ cup buttermilk
2 tablespoons milk

Preheat oven to 400°F.

Combine the pastry flour, wheat bran, wheat germ, oat bran, baking powder, and baking soda. Stir in the mixed herbs.

With a pastry blender or two knives, cut in the butter until the mixture is the consistency of coarse cornmeal. Make a well in the center of the ingredients and add the buttermilk all at once. Work the dough with your hands until it comes free from the sides of the bowl for a scant ½ minute. Gather up pieces the size of a walnut, roll into a ball, and place in 24 paper minimuffin cups. Brush the tops with milk and bake for 10 minutes.

Yield: 2 dozen minimuffins.

Approximately 38 calories each.

Pineapple Apricot Minimuffins

We make these small because they are so richly satisfying. Vary the garnish and one batch will provide an appetizing variety of tastes.

½ cup wheat bran
¾ cup buttermilk or yogurt
3 eggs
2 tablespoons olive oil
2 tablespoons honey
10 dried apricots presoaked in
    ½ cup boiling water
1 tablespoon grated orange
    rind
¾ cup shredded pineapple,
    drained
¼ cup soy flour

2 cups sifted whole wheat
    flour
¼ cup oat bran
½ cup wheat germ
2 teaspoons baking powder
1 teaspoon baking soda
½ cup sunflower seeds or
    chopped walnuts
sliced almonds, pecans,
    walnuts, or coconut for
    garnish

Soak the bran in the buttermilk or yogurt. Set aside.

In a mixing bowl or food processor, blend together the eggs, olive oil, honey, soaked apricots with their liquid, the orange rind, the pineapple, and the bran mixture.

In another bowl, combine the flours, oat bran, wheat germ, baking powder, baking soda, and sunflower seeds or walnuts.

Preheat oven to 350°F. Insert 4 dozen minicups into muffin tins and fill halfway. Garnish with sliced almonds, walnuts, pecans, coconut, or some of each.

Yield: 4 dozen minimuffins.

Approximately 40 calories each.

Ambrosia Muffins

These heavenly minimuffins, flavored with orange, pineapple, and coconut, are festive enough for a party, easy enough for everyday enjoyment, and very rich in fiber, calcium, magnesium, and potassium.

1 cup wheat bran
1 cup pineapple juice
3 medium-size eggs
2 tablespoons olive oil or
    softened unsalted butter
2 tablespoons honey or
    molasses
½ cup frozen orange juice
    concentrate (slightly
    thawed)

2 cups sifted whole wheat
    flour
2 tablespoons milk powder
¼ cup oat bran
¼ cup lecithin granules
2 teaspoons baking powder
1 teaspoon baking soda
1 cup shredded coconut
½ cup coarsely chopped
    walnuts

Soak the wheat bran in the pineapple juice and set aside. In a mixing bowl or food processor, blend together the eggs, oil or butter, honey or molasses, and orange juice concentrate. Add the pineapple-bran mixture.

In a bowl, combine the wheat flour, milk powder, oat bran, lecithin granules, baking powder, and baking soda.

Preheat oven to 350°F. Grease 4 dozen minimuffin tins with a lecithin and oil mixture, or line them with paper or foil muffin cups.

Add the dry ingredients to the wet mixture and mix only to blend. Stir in the coconut and walnuts.

Fill the muffin cups ¾ full and bake about 15 to 20 minutes or until golden brown.

Yield: 4 dozen minimuffins.

Approximately 54 calories each.

Cranberry Banana Nut Muffins

These wholesome, high-fiber muffins are a lovely accompaniment to any meal you give thanks for. Both bananas and cranberries are very high in potassium and low in sodium. Cranberries contribute magnesium, sulfur, chlorine, iron, and maganese, a mineral needed for the manufacture of cartilage.

2 eggs
3 tablespoons olive oil or
  softened butter
3 tablespoons honey
3 tablespoons molasses
3 tablespoons orange juice
  concentrate
1 teaspoon vanilla
1 cup mashed banana
1 cup chopped cranberries

½ cup chopped nuts
1 cup sifted whole wheat flour
2 tablespoons wheat bran
2 tablespoons wheat germ
¼ cup oat bran
1 tablespoon grated orange
  rind
½ teaspoon baking powder
½ teaspoon baking soda
  flaked coconut for garnish

In a large mixing bowl or food processor, blend together the eggs, oil or butter, honey, molasses, orange juice concentrate, vanilla extract, and mashed banana. Add the chopped cranberries and nuts.

In another bowl, combine the wheat flour, wheat bran, wheat germ, oat bran, orange rind, baking powder, and baking soda.

Preheat oven to 375°F. Line with paper cups or grease 3 dozen minimuffin cups or 1 dozen regular muffin cups. Spoon the batter into the cups, top with a sprinkling of coconut, and bake the minimuffins for 15 minutes—regular size for 20 to 25 minutes—or until golden and crusty.

Yield: 3 dozen minimuffins or 1 dozen regular-size muffins.

Approximately 55 calories each for minimuffins, approximately 166 calories each for regular-size muffins.

3

EAT-YOUR-VEGETABLES MUFFINS

Put on your thinking cap and get ready for a little trivia. What class of foods meets all the criteria for the ideal food plan—high complex carbohydrates, high fiber, high mineral and vitamin content, low fat, and low in calories?

The answer, of course, is *vegetables.*

And now, with the exciting recent studies showing the value of beta carotene as a substance that helps retard and even prevent the development of cancerous growths, the push is on to get more vegetables into our diet.

But what about taste? Many of us still harbor memories of tired, tasteless blobs of vegetables that we were coaxed to eat because there were starving children in India. And mothers across the country are still nudging and threatening, "Eat your carrots or you don't get dessert!"

The answer is to make vegetables so appealing that children will prefer them to dessert. How? Make great vegetable muffins! Carrots, sweet potatoes, zucchini, cauliflower, and peppers never tasted so good.

Here are some tips on how to select the freshest and most flavorful vegetables for your muffins:

Carrots: Look for carrots that are well formed, smooth, bright orange, and firm. Avoid roots with large green "sunburned" areas at the top. These must be cut away. And watch out for roots that are flabby or that show spots of decay.

Peppers: Look for a glossy sheen, firm walls, and a relatively heavy weight. Avoid peppers with very thin walls (they will be lighter and have flimsy sides) and those that are wilted or flabby with cuts or punctures through the walls.

Sweet potatoes: Look for well-shaped, firm sweet potatoes with smooth, bright, uniformly colored skins free from signs of decay. Avoid those with worm holes, cuts, or any other defects that penetrate the skin; these cause decay. Even if you cut away the decayed portion, the remainder of the sweet potato, though it looks normal, may have a bad taste. Store sweet potatoes in a cool, dark, dry place but not in the refrigerator.

Zucchini and other members of the squash family: Look for ones that are well developed, firm and brightly colored, with no brown patches. The skin should be glossy and not hard or tough. Avoid overmature squash with a dull appearance and a hard, tough surface.

Don't buy vegetables from the bargain basket. It's penny-foolish. A few cents extra for vegetables in top condition is a good investment.

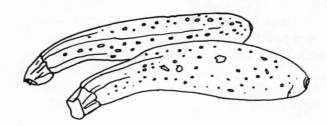

Cauliflower Muffins

These muffins add pizzazz and many health benefits to a fish or fowl dinner or, topped with melted cheese, they make a satisfying lunch. Cauliflower—known as the cabbage that went to college—is a member of the brassica or cabbage patch family, which was recently found to provide a measure of protection against cancer of the colon. Besides providing potassium, calcium, and vitamins A, the B's, and C, cauliflower also is a dieter's delight—only 49 calories in 1½ cups. Eggs are a good source of selenium, a mineral used in the treatment of cancer.

1 large head of cauliflower, trimmed and separated into flowerettes
1 medium-size onion, diced
3 eggs
¼ teaspoon white pepper
¼ teaspoon nutmeg

2 tablespoons wheat germ or whole wheat flour
2 tablespoons oat bran
2 tablespoons lecithin granules
3 tablespoons olive oil
sesame seeds for garnish

In a food processor, using a metal blade, combine the cauliflower, onion, eggs, pepper, and nutmeg. Process until the cauliflower is finely chopped. Add the rest of the ingredients except the sesame seeds, and process briefly.

Preheat oven to 375°F. Grease 12 regular-size muffin wells with a mixture of liquid lecithin and oil, or line them with foil baking cups. Spoon the batter into the muffin cups. Sprinkle sesame seeds on top of each muffin. Bake for 25 to 30 minutes or until the tops are golden. Serve with applesauce or yogurt.

Yield: 12 muffins.

Approximately 65 calories each.

Carrot Orange Pecan Muffins

Orange concentrate and plumped raisins combine with grated carrots to bring sweetness and many palate-pleasing textures and flavors to these nutritious muffins. Carrots are loaded with vitamin A (15,600 I.U. in a cup), needed for growth and repair of body tissue. It also helps fight infection and promotes a smooth, blemish-free complexion.

2 eggs
½ cup frozen orange juice
    concentrate
3 tablespoons olive oil,
    vegetable oil, or
    softened butter
¼ cup buttermilk or yogurt
1½ cups grated carrot (½
    pound)
½ cup chopped pecans
½ cup plumped raisins
1¼ cups sifted whole wheat
    flour

¼ cup wheat germ
2 tablespoons lecithin granules
2 tablespoons oat bran
1 teaspoon cinnamon
1 tablespoon grated orange
    rind
½ teaspoon ginger
1 teaspoon baking soda
1 teaspoon baking powder
    shredded coconut for
    garnish

In a large bowl or food processor, blend together the eggs, orange juice concentrate, oil or butter, buttermilk or yogurt, and grated carrots. Mix in the raisins and nuts.

In another bowl, stir together the flour, wheat germ, lecithin granules, oat bran, cinnamon, orange rind, ginger, baking soda, and baking powder.

Preheat oven to 375°F. Grease or line with paper or foil cups 3 dozen minimuffin cups or 1 dozen regular-size tins.

Add the dry ingredients to the wet mixture and blend together briefly, only enough to combine. Spoon the mixture into the prepared cups; top with coconut and bake for 15 minutes.

Yield: 3 dozen minimuffins or 1 dozen regular-size muffins.

Approximately 47 calories each for minimuffins, approximately 141 calories each for regular-size muffins.

Zucchini Raisin and Nut Muffins

Don't despair if the children make a meal of these high-protein, very nutritious, deliciously moist muffins. Zucchini is rich in vitamin A and potassium and incredibly low in calories. So enjoy them in good conscience.

½ cup raisins
2 cups grated unpeeled zucchini
2 eggs
3 tablespoons olive or vegetable oil, or softened butter
¼ cup honey
1 teaspoon vanilla
1½ cups sifted whole wheat pastry flour
¼ cup soy flour
¼ cup oatmeal
2 tablespoons wheat germ
2 tablespoons oat bran
2 tablespoons wheat bran
2 teaspoons baking powder
1 teaspoon baking soda
1 teaspoon cinnamon
2 teaspoons grated orange rind
½ cup chopped walnuts or pecans

Combine the raisins and grated zucchini. Set aside.

In a mixing bowl or food processor, blend together the eggs, oil or butter, honey, and vanilla. Add the zucchini-raisin mixture.

In another bowl, mix together the flours, oatmeal, wheat germ, oat bran, wheat bran, baking powder, baking soda, cinnamon, and orange rind.

Preheat oven to 400°F. Grease 12 regular-size muffin cups with a lecithin and oil mixture or line with baking cups.

Add the dry ingredients to the wet mixture and blend together only until all the flour is moistened. Stir in the nuts. Fill the muffin cups with batter and bake for about 20 minutes.

Yield: 12 large muffins.

Approximately 189 calories each.

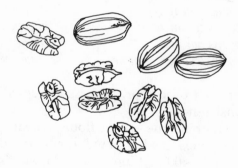

Potato Muffins

These savory, crisp-crusted muffins are a perfect accompaniment for a wonderful chicken dinner. Potatoes are an excellent source of energy, high in fiber, and believe it or not, low in calories—only 90 calories in a 5-ounce potato, which also provides 20 milligrams of vitamin C.

3 eggs
1 medium-size onion, diced
2 large unpeeled potatoes,
    scrubbed and diced
¼ cup whole wheat flour
2 tablespoons wheat germ
2 tablespoons wheat bran
2 tablespoons oat bran
2 tablespoons lecithin granules

½ teaspoon baking powder
¼ teaspoon cinnamon
⅛ teaspoon curry
½ teaspoon freshly ground
    pepper
2 tablespoons fresh dill
    snipped or 1 teaspoon
    dried
sesame seeds for garnish

In a blender or food processor, process the eggs, onion, and potatoes to a coarse consistency.

In a bowl, combine the wheat flour, wheat germ, wheat and oat bran, lecithin granules, baking powder, cinnamon, curry, and pepper.

Preheat oven to 400°F. Line 12 regular-size muffin tins with foil cups.

Add the dry ingredients to the potato mixture and process to blend all the ingredients. Stir in the dill.

Spoon the batter into the muffin cups and top with a sprinkle of sesame seeds. Bake for 25 to 30 minutes or until the muffins are toasty brown.

Yield: 12 muffins.

Approximately 65 calories each.

Orange Parsnip Snowballs

Sweet parsnips accented with tangy orange juice, golden raisins, crunchy coconut, and pecans or walnuts make these muffins deliciousy wholesome. Parsnips provide more potassium and more calcium than bananas. Coconut provides potassium, iron, and traces of the B vitamins.

1 cup grated parsnip (1 large or 2 small)
⅓ cup frozen orange juice concentrate
½ cup orange juice
2 eggs
3 tablespoons olive or vegetable oil
3 tablespoons honey
½ cup golden raisins, plumped
1½ cups sifted whole wheat pastry flour
½ cup rolled oats
3 tablespoons wheat germ
1 teaspoon baking soda
1 teaspoon baking powder
1 teaspoon cinnamon
1 tablespoon grated orange rind
½ cup chopped pecans or walnuts
flaked, unsweetened coconut for garnish

In a mixing bowl or food processor, blend together the grated parsnip, orange juice concentrate and juice, eggs, oil, and honey. Stir in the raisins.

In another bowl, mix together the flour, oats, wheat germ, baking soda, baking powder, cinnamon, and orange rind.

Preheat oven to 400°F. Grease 12 regular-size muffin cups with a lecithin and oil mixture. Sprinkle coconut in each muffin cup.

Add the dry ingredients to the parsnip mixture and blend only until no flour is visible. Stir in the nuts.

NOTE: To grate the parsnip, scrub it well but do not peel. Use a hand grater or food processor, using a steel blade.

Spoon the batter into the muffin cups. Top each muffin with a sprinkle of coconut. Bake for 18 to 20 minutes.

Yield: 12 muffins.

Approximately 191 calories each.

Lemony Squash Muffins

When your garden or marketplace is overflowing with squash, make these muffins and freeze them to enjoy the sweet taste of summer when snow covers the ground. Squash is rich in beta carotene, found recently to be a cancer deterrent.

2 cups grated yellow squash
½ cup plumped raisins
2 tablespoons lemon juice or pulp
3 tablespoons maple syrup
2 eggs
1½ cups sifted whole wheat pastry flour
¼ cup wheat germ

2 teaspoons baking powder
½ teaspoon baking soda
1 teaspoon cinnamon
¼ teaspoon ginger
1 tablespoon grated lemon rind
½ cup chopped walnuts, pecans, or peanuts
sunflower seeds for garnish

In a mixing bowl or food processor, blend together the squash, raisins, lemon juice or pulp, maple syrup, and eggs.

In another bowl, combine the pastry flour, wheat germ, baking powder, baking soda, cinnamon, ginger, and lemon rind.

Preheat oven to 400°F. Grease 12 regular-size muffin tins with a lecithin and oil mixture.

Add the dry ingredients to the squash mixture and process briefly, only until all the flour is moistened. Stir in the nuts.

Spoon the batter into the muffin tins. Top each muffin with a few sunflower seeds. Bake 18 to 20 minutes.

Yield: 12 muffins.

Approximately 133 calories each.

Remarkable Yellow Pepper Muffins

Yellow peppers are incredibly sweet and nutrient-dense, providing more vitamin C than most oranges, lots of carotene, potassium, vitamin A, some calcium, iron, and the vitamin B's. And they're ridiculously low in calories. Flax seed is a rich source of omega 3 fatty acids, the kind that are good for your heart and arteries.

1 cup diced yellow pepper	3 tablespoons wheat germ
1 egg	2 tablespoons oat bran
1 tablespoon olive or vegetable oil	1 tablespoon flax seed
2 tablespoons honey	1 tablespoon grated orange rind
1 tablespoon molasses	1 teaspoon cinnamon
½ cup buttermilk or yogurt	⅛ teaspoon nutmeg
1 cup whole wheat pastry flour	pinch of ginger
2 tablespoons wheat bran	½ cup currants
	¼ cup chopped walnuts

Purée the pepper in a food processor, using a metal blade.

Add to the puréed pepper the egg, oil, honey, molasses, and buttermilk or yogurt, and process to blend all the ingredients.

In another bowl, combine the pastry flour, wheat bran, wheat germ, oat bran, flax seed, orange rind, cinnamon, nutmeg, and ginger.

Preheat oven to 400°F. Line 12 regular-size muffin wells with foil or paper baking cups, or grease with a mixture of oil and lecithin.

Combine the wet and dry mixtures and mix briefly just to blend

the ingredients. Stir in the currants and walnuts. Spoon the batter
into the muffin wells and bake for 18 to 20 minutes.
Yield: 12 muffins.
Approximately 105 calories each.

Sweet Potato Maple Walnut Muffins

What a delightful way to get your beta carotene and your potassium
in every delicious bite, plus a good helping of precious linoleic acid,
which helps prevent harmful deposits of cholesterol and contributes
to smooth, beautiful skin.

> 2 eggs
> ⅓ cup maple syrup
> 2 tablespoons sweet butter or
>   olive oil
> ½ cup crushed, unsweetened
>   pineapple with juice
> 1 teaspoon vanilla
> 1 cup grated raw sweet potato

> ½ cup raisins, plumped
> ½ cup sunflower seeds or
>   chopped walnuts
> 1¾ cups sifted whole wheat flour
> ¼ cup wheat germ
> 2 teaspoons baking powder
> 1 teaspoon cinnamon
> ⅛ teaspoon ground nutmeg

In a large bowl or food processor, blend together the eggs, maple
syrup, butter or olive oil, pineapple, vanilla, sweet potato, raisins,
and walnuts or sunflower seeds.

In another bowl, stir together the wheat flour, wheat germ, baking powder, cinnamon, and nutmeg.

Preheat oven to 375°F. Grease or line 3 dozen minimuffin wells or 1 dozen regular-size muffin wells.

Combine the wet and dry ingredients and mix only enough to combine the ingredients. Spoon the mixture into the prepared muffin tins. Sprinkle a few nuts or seeds on each muffin.

Bake 12 to 15 minutes for minimuffins, 20 to 25 minutes for regular-size muffins or until golden brown and a cake tester comes out clean.

Yield: 3 dozen minimuffins or 1 dozen regular-size muffins.

Approximately 50 calories each for minimuffins, approximately 179 calories each for regular-size muffins.

Herbed Corn Muffins

Irresistibly good with fish or fowl. Serve them hot and crunchy. They freeze well, so you can make them way ahead of the holiday rush. The oat bran contributes high-density lipoprotein that protects the arteries from arteriosclerosis.

2 eggs
1 cup buttermilk
1 tablespoon honey
¼ cup melted butter
1 well-packed tablespoon
    minced fresh sage or 1
    teaspoon dried
3 tablespoons minced fresh
    dill or 3 teaspoons dried

1 cup cornmeal
1 cup whole wheat pastry flour
2 tablespoons oat bran
2 tablespoons lecithin granules
    sesame or poppy seeds for
    garnish

In a mixing bowl or food processor, blend together the eggs, buttermilk, honey, and butter. Add the minced herbs.

In another bowl, mix together the cornmeal, pastry flour, oat bran, and lecithin granules.

Preheat oven to 400°F. Butter 12 regular-size muffin cups.

Combine the dry and wet ingredients and blend together only until no flour is visible. Fill each muffin cup ¾ full. Top with poppy or sesame seeds—or both. Bake for 12 minutes and enjoy the savory fragrance.

Yield: 12 muffins.

Approximately 144 calories each.

4

MEALS-IN-A-MUFFIN

You'll love having a supply of these savory muffins in the freezer. On days when you'd rather go to the gym, to the pool, or shopping, than cook a complete dinner, you'll be thankful to have these splendid, ready-to-eat meals right at your fingertips.

I consider these muffins great stress-breakers. One of the biggest stresses we face is figuring out what to have for dinner, what to bring to the covered dish supper, what to prepare for a condolence call, and what to make for the new family on the block. With these Meals-in-a-Muffin, you'll be armed for any occasion.

Meals-in-a-Muffin also provide you with an easy and delicious way to recycle your leftovers. Using these recipes as your guide, you can turn leftover potatoes, broccoli, and even holiday turkey into scrumptious muffins to enjoy now or later.

The Tuna Melt Muffins and the Pizza Muffins are favorites with my grandchildren. When they barge in, cold and hungry after a long trip, I pop a tray of these muffins into the oven and have them ready by the time the kids have hugged everybody and hung up their coats.

Zesty Black Bean and Rice Muffins

Marvelous for a cocktail party or as an appetizer to heighten your dining experience. The combination of black beans and rice was introduced to us by Carla, our Brazilian daughter, who spent a year with us as an exchange student. She liked to put slices of banana on top for a contrast in flavor. Beans and rice have complementary amino acids, making the combination a complete protein.

1 cup cooked black turtle
   beans
1 cup brown rice
¼ cup chopped fresh parsley
½ teaspoon curry powder
1 clove garlic, crushed

1 tablespoon tamari soy sauce
1 small egg
2 tablespoons sunflower seeds
   ground to a flour
½ to ¾ cup sesame seeds

In a mixing bowl, combine all the ingredients except the sesame seeds. Mix well with a fork.

Preheat oven to 350°F and line a 2-dozen minimuffin tin with paper or foil liners.

Form the mixture into walnut-size balls and roll in the sesame seeds. Place the balls in the muffin cups and bake for 10 to 15 minutes. These can be served hot or cold.

Yield: 2 dozen minimuffins.

Approximately 46 calories each.

Hearty Macaroni and Cheese Muffins

These muffins are perfect for a festive brunch, as a side dish for a fish or vegetarian meal, or with a salad. They freeze well but, to savor their zesty flavors, serve them hot. Cottage cheese is high in protein, calcium, and selenium, the remarkable nutrient that combats aging.

2 cups cooked elbow macaroni (preferably whole wheat)
1 cup cottage cheese
1 egg, lightly beaten
½ cup milk
2 tablespoons wheat germ
1 tablespoon grated onion
1 tablespoon chopped chives

½ teaspoon dry mustard
¼ to ½ teaspoon freshly ground pepper
2 tablespoons bran
2 tablespoons sesame seeds
mozzarella or cheddar cheese for topping

Preheat oven to 350°F. Line 6 regular-size muffin wells with foil liners.

In a medium-size mixing bowl, combine the macaroni, cottage cheese, egg, milk, wheat germ, onion, chives, mustard, and pepper.

Spoon the mixture into the muffin cups and insert strips of cheese into each muffin. Combine the bran and sesame seeds. Sprinkle this mix on the muffins.

Yield: 6 muffins.

Approximately 126 calories each.

Blintz Muffins

Served fresh from the oven or at room temperature, these high-protein muffins and a salad make a satisfying meal. They also make a substantial lunch box treat. Eggs are an excellent source of protein, vitamins A, B, E, and K, and are one of the few foods that provide vitamin D, so essential to the utilization of calcium.

3 eggs
1 cup cottage cheese
3 tablespoons sour cream
2 tablespoons honey
1 teaspoon vanilla
½ cup whole wheat pastry
   flour

2 tablespoons wheat germ
2 tablespoons lecithin granules
1 tablespoon grated orange
   rind
½ teaspoon cinnamon
   sliced almonds for garnish

In a mixing bowl or food processor, blend together the eggs, cheese, sour cream, honey, and vanilla.

In another bowl, combine the pastry flour, wheat germ, lecithin granules, orange rind, and cinnamon.

Preheat oven to 350°F. Grease 12 regular-size muffin cups, or 3 dozen minicups, or line with foil baking cups.

Spoon the batter into the cups. Top each muffin with a few slices of almonds. Bake regular-size muffins for 25 minutes, minimuffins for 15 to 18 minutes.

Yield: 12 regular-size muffins or 36 minimuffins.

Approximately 73 calories each for regular-size muffins, approximately 24 calories each for minimuffins.

Pizza Muffins

You simply must try these muffins. They rise up high and look gorgeous in their tomato and cheese top hats. The kids go gaga for them. To serve, split them in halves and serve hot and topped with mozzarella cheese.

1 egg
½ cup tomato sauce
1 cup buttermilk or yogurt
4 slices mozzarella cheese, cut in dice
¼ teaspoon freshly ground pepper
1 teaspoon crushed dry oregano leaf

¼ teaspoon garlic powder
1½ cups whole wheat pastry flour
3 tablespoons wheat germ
2 teaspoons baking powder
1 teaspoon baking soda
sliced tomatoes and more cheese for garnish
sesame seeds

In a mixing bowl or food processor, blend together the egg, tomato sauce, and buttermilk or yogurt. Add the cheese and the spices. In another bowl, mix together the pastry flour, wheat germ, baking powder, and baking soda.

Preheat oven to 400°F. Butter or grease with a lecithin and oil mixture 12 regular-size muffin cups.

Combine the two mixtures and mix until no flour is visible. Spoon the batter into the muffin cups and top each muffin with a slice of tomato, cover it with cheese, and sprinkle sesame seeds on top. Bake for 20 to 25 minutes.

Yield: 12 muffins.

Approximately 88 calories each.

Mushroom Broccoli Cheese Muffins

Broccoli is the most nutrient-dense food in the marketplace, with twice as much vitamin C as orange juice and with potassium, lots of calcium and vitamin A, and some B vitamins. All this goodness at a cost of only 26 calories in 3½ ounces. Even vegetable-scorners flip for these nutrient-rich, low-calorie treats.

2 cups lightly steamed chopped broccoli	2 eggs
½ cup grated cheddar or mozzarella cheese	3 tablespoons wheat germ
½ cup chopped onions	4 tablespoons whole wheat flour
1 cup chopped mushrooms	¼ teaspoon pepper
2 tablespoons butter	1 teaspoon crushed leaf oregano
2 tablespoons whole wheat pastry flour	sesame seeds and more cheese for garnish
½ cup water	

Combine the broccoli and the cheese and set aside. Sauté the onions and mushrooms in the butter. Stir in the 2 tablespoons of pastry flour and add the water. Cook slowly until the sauce thickens.

In a mixing bowl or food processor, blend together the eggs, wheat germ, remaining flour, pepper, and oregano.

Preheat oven to 400°F. Butter or grease with a lecithin and oil mixture 12 regular-size muffin cups. Sprinkle sesame seeds on the bottom of each.

Combine the broccoli-cheese mixture with the other mixture. Spoon into the muffin cups. Top each with a sprinkle of sesame seeds and cheese. Bake for 20 minutes.

Yield: 12 muffins.

Approximately 91 calories each.

Hearty Kasha Mushroom Cheese Muffins

Kasha is roasted buckwheat groats. It looks like a grain but is not. It is related to the rhubarb family, has a hearty flavor, and is an excellent source of iron. Mushrooms help you to cope. They are rich in pantothenic acid, the antistress vitamin.

1 medium onion, chopped
1 cup chopped mushrooms
1 cup chopped zucchini
    (optional)
1 tablespoon butter
1 cup cooked kasha (buck-
    wheat groats)
2 eggs, beaten
½ cup cottage cheese
¼ cup wheat germ
¼ cup whole wheat pastry
    flour

½ teaspoon baking powder
½ teaspoon curry powder
1 teaspoon dried thyme or 1
    tablespoon fresh
1 teaspoon vegetable season-
    ing or to taste
grated cheddar cheese, sliced
    almonds, and paprika
    for garnish

Sauté the onion, mushrooms, and zucchini in the butter. Mix in the kasha, cottage cheese, and eggs.

In another bowl, combine the wheat germ, pastry flour, baking powder, curry powder, thyme, and vegetable seasoning.

Preheat oven to 400°F. Grease 12 regular-size muffin tins with butter or a lecithin and oil mixture.

Combine the wet and dry mixtures. Stir briefly to blend. Spoon the batter into the muffin cups. Sprinkle with cheese, paprika, and almonds. Bake for 20 minutes.

Yield: 12 muffins.

Approximately 74 calories each.

Corny Potato Sunflower Muffins

These are a must for holiday meals. The aroma as they are baking raises the cockles on appetites. They taste like knishes. Potatoes are a good source of fiber. Serve them piping hot.

2 medium-size onions, chopped
½ cup sunflower seeds
1 tablespoon butter or oil
1 cup corn niblets
2 cups mashed potatoes
2 eggs

¼ cup whole wheat pastry flour
¼ cup wheat germ
¼ teaspoon baking powder
½ teaspoon freshly grated pepper
¼ teaspoon grated nutmeg
sprinkle of paprika

Sauté the onions and sunflower seeds in the butter or oil. Add the corn.

In a bowl, combine the mashed potatoes, 1 egg, and 1 egg white. Reserve the other yolk.

Combine the pastry flour, wheat germ, and baking powder and add to the mashed potatoes. Combine this mixture with the onion mixture. Add the spices.

Preheat oven to 400°F. Grease 12 muffin cups with a lecithin and oil mixture.

Spoon the mixture into the muffin cups. Brush each muffin with egg yolk. Bake for 20 minutes or until golden brown.

Yield: 12 muffins.

Approximately 105 calories each.

Corny Corn and Chive Muffins

Serve these muffins hot with a hearty bowl of soup or chowder and you've got a meal. Corn is low in fat, high in fiber, and provides potassium, vitamin A, and niacin, which tends to lower cholesterol.

2 eggs
1 cup buttermilk or yogurt
2 tablespoons softened butter
    or olive or vegetable oil
2 tablespoons minced fresh
    chives or 2 teaspoons
    dried
1 cup corn, scraped from a
    cooked cob, or frozen
    corn, thawed, or canned
    corn, drained

1½ cups yellow cornmeal
¼ cup whole wheat flour
2 tablespoons wheat germ
2 tablespoons wheat or oat
    bran
1 tablespoon baking powder
1 teaspoon baking soda
    mozzarella or cheddar
    cheese and sesame seeds
    for garnish

In a mixing bowl or food processor, blend the eggs, buttermilk or yogurt, butter or oil, and the chives. Add the corn kernels.

In another bowl, combine the cornmeal, flour, wheat germ, bran, baking powder, and baking soda.

Preheat oven to 400°F. Grease 12 regular-size muffin cups with a lecithin and oil mixture or line with foil baking cups.

Spoon 2 tablespoons of batter into each cup. Place a piece of cheese on each, then the rest of the batter on top of the cheese. Place another small piece of cheese on top of each muffin and top with a sprinkle of sesame seeds. Bake for 20 minutes.

Yield: 12 muffins.

Approximately 123 calories each.

Bird's Nest Pineapple Noodle Muffins

These miniature kugels go great with chicken or fish and double as dessert. Pineapple provides protective vitamins A and C and an enzyme that helps digest protein.

8 ounces fine noodles
2 quarts boiling water
1 can (20 ounces) crushed
    pineapple (drained);
    reserve juice
2 tablespoons bran soaked in 4
    tablespoons of the
    pineapple juice

4 eggs
2 tablespoons honey
¼ cup wheat germ
2 tablespoons lecithin granules
½ cup raisins, plumped
    sunflower seeds for garnish

Cook the noodles in boiling water for about 8 minutes or until *al dente*. Drain. Drain the pineapple in a colander set over a bowl. In a small bowl, soak the bran in the pineapple juice. In another bowl or in a food processor, beat the eggs, then add the honey, wheat germ, lecithin granules, and raisins. Mix to blend all these ingredients.

In a large bowl, combine the drained noodles, the soaked bran, and the egg mixture.

Preheat oven to 375°F. Grease 24 regular-size muffin cups with a lecithin and oil mixture. Spoon the noodle mixture into the muffin cups. Top each with a few sunflower seeds and bake for 25 to 30 minutes or until golden brown.

Yield: 2 dozen muffins.
Approximately 79 calories each.

Matzo Meal Muffins

Eggs are the only leavening in these muffins, which are acceptable for Passover but welcome anytime. Serve hot with butter, cream cheese, or fruit conserve, or plain, dunked in chicken soup.

3 eggs, separated
1 tablespoon grated orange rind

1 cup cold water
1½ cups matzo meal

In a mixing bowl or mixing machine, beat the egg whites until they form peaks. Continue beating as you dribble in the egg yolks.

Add the orange rind to the matzo meal. Add the matzo meal mixture and water alternately to the beaten eggs.

Preheat oven to 400°F. Line 12 regular-size muffin wells with foil baking cups or grease with oil.

Spoon the batter into the muffin wells and bake for about 30 minutes or until a cake tester comes out clean.

Yield: 12 muffins.

Approximately 76 calories each.

Variation: Use chicken broth instead of water and serve with chicken soup.

Tuna Apple Almond Muffins

Here's a versatile muffin. Terrific for lunch boxes, wholesome after-school snacks, wonderful for buffets, and a welcome bring-along dish. Oats and oat bran have been shown to lower cholesterol levels.

1 6½- or 7-ounce can tuna
    packed in water, drained
½ cup finely chopped celery
½ cup chopped apple
½ cup rolled oats (preferably
    uncooked)
2 tablespoons oat bran

½ cup chopped, roasted
    almonds or sunflower
    seeds
2 eggs, lightly beaten
⅛ teaspoon pepper
½ cup milk

DILL SAUCE

½ cup plain yogurt
½ cup chopped cucumber
2 tablespoons chopped fresh
    dill or 1 teaspoon dried

1 teaspoon minced onion

To make the sauce: In a small bowl, combine all ingredients and mix well. Chill.

To make the muffins: In a medium-size bowl, blend the tuna, then add the celery, apple, oats and oat bran, almonds or sunflower seeds, eggs, pepper, and milk.

Preheat oven to 350°F. Line 12 regular-size muffin wells with foil liners.

Spoon the batter into the muffin wells and bake for 20 to 25 minutes. Serve warm, cold, or hot from the oven with dill sauce.
Yield: 12 muffins.
Approximately 100 calories each with 2 tablespoons of sauce, approximately 98 calories each without sauce.

Turkey Cranberry Almond Muffins

I always plan to have turkey or chicken left over so I can treat my family to these crunchy, wholesome muffins. I serve them in good consience because they provide high-quality protein, plenty of the vitamin B's, and flavor that puts a smile on every face.

¼ to ½ cup turkey gravy
1 cup chopped onions
1 cup chopped celery
2 cloves garlic, minced
2 tablespoons chopped parsley
4 fresh sage leaves, chopped, or ¼ teaspoon dry sage
1½ cups turkey, cut in bite-size pieces
1 cup cooked brown rice
1 cup chopped roasted almonds

1 egg, beaten
a piece of ginger, dry mustard, and nutmeg
½ teaspoon curry powder
½ teaspoon dried thyme
¼ cup cranberry sauce conserve (Sorrell Ridge, unsweetened) or your own cranberry sauce
1 mellow banana, mashed (optional)

Heat a large skillet, add the gravy, and sauté the onions and celery. Add the garlic, parsley, sage, turkey, rice, almonds, egg, spices, and cranberry sauce (banana can be added if desired).

Preheat oven to 350°F. Line regular-size muffin wells with foil baking cups. Spoon the batter into the cups, top each with a dab of cranberry sauce, and bake for 20 minutes.

Yield: 12 muffins.

Approximately 130 calories each.

Tuna Melt Muffins

Teenagers flip for these. They love to find them all ready for the toaster on days when you can't be there to greet them. Tuna provides more protein than an equal amount of porterhouse steak and is much kinder on your arteries and your budget.

1 tablespoon butter
1 tablespoon olive or vegetable oil
1 medium-size onion, minced
2 stalks celery, diced, about 1 cup
1 green or red pepper, diced
½ cup chopped almonds
¼ cup minced fresh parsley
2 cans water-packed tuna fish (6½ or 7 ounces each)
2 tablespoons lemon juice

2 eggs, beaten
½ cup sour cream or yogurt
½ cup whole wheat pastry flour
3 tablespoons wheat germ
2 tablespoons oat bran
2 tablespoons lecithin granules
1 teaspoon baking powder
¼ teaspoon freshly ground pepper
mozzarella cheese for topping

In a large skillet, heat the butter and oil. Sauté the onion briefly, then add the celery, pepper, and almonds. Add the parsley when the other ingredients are almost completely sautéed.

In another bowl, mix together the tuna, lemon juice, eggs, sour cream or yogurt, pastry flour, wheat germ, oat bran, lecithin granules, baking powder, and pepper.

Preheat oven to 375°F. Grease 12 regular-size muffin cups with a butter or lecithin and oil mixture.

Combine the tuna mixture with the sautéed ingredients. Spoon the mixture into the muffin cups. Top each muffin with a piece of cheese. Bake for 20 minutes.

Yield: 12 muffins.

Approximately 170 calories each.

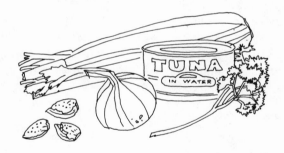

Salmon Rice Almond Muffins

Serve these muffins hot with yogurt dill sauce for a delectable main dish. Brown rice is a wonderful source of complex carbohydrates for energy and stamina. Salmon is a good source of Maz EPA, the poly-unsaturated fat that lowers cholesterol levels in the blood.

1 egg
¼ cup yogurt
1 small onion, chopped or grated if you're not using a processor
2 small potatoes, parboiled in their jackets, mashed if you're not using a food processor
1 7½-ounce can salmon with bones and skin or ¾ to 1 cup flaked salmon left over from dinner

1 cup cooked brown rice
2 tablespoons chopped fresh dill or 2 teaspoons dried
¼ teaspoon freshly ground pepper
grating of nutmeg
2 tablespoons whole wheat flour
2 tablespoons wheat germ
½ teaspoon baking soda
½ cup slivered almonds sesame seeds, cheese, and paprika for garnish

In a mixing bowl or food processor, blend together the egg, yogurt, onion, potatoes, salmon, rice, dill, pepper, and nutmeg. Stir in the rice.

In another bowl, combine the flour, wheat germ, baking soda, and almonds.

Preheat oven to 375°F. Line 12 muffin cups with foil baking cups or grease with a mixture of lecithin and oil.

Combine the salmon mixture and the flour mixture. Mix only until the dry ingredients are moistened. Spoon the mixture into the muffin cups. Top with sesame seeds and cheese, and dust with paprika. Bake for 25 to 30 minutes or until golden brown.

Yield: 12 muffins.

Approximately 120 calories each.

Variation: Use haddock, scrod, cod, or any fish you can salvage from dinner. I always buy more than I need for dinner so I have enough left over for these muffins.

Vegetarian Meal-in-a-Muffin

Tofu and brown rice team up with crisp vegetables and walnuts for a delectable oriental flavor. Two of these muffins with a salad make a satisfying, high-energy meal. Tofu (derived from soybeans) is high in protein without the fat that usually accompanies high-protein foods. Tofu also provides lecithin and choline, both of which jog the memory.

1 to 2 tablespoons olive or vegetable oil
1 cup tofu, cut in dice
1 cup chopped onion
1 cup chopped celery
1 cup chopped zucchini
2 large cloves of garlic, minced
½ cup chopped walnuts
1 cup cooked brown rice
1 egg plus one egg yolk
2 teaspoons brown rice vinegar

3 tablespoons tamari soy sauce
2 teaspoons lemon juice
¼ teaspoon ground ginger or more to taste
3 tablespoons brown rice polish or flour
2 tablespoons sesame seeds slivered almonds or whole cashews for garnish

In a large skillet or wok, heat the oil and sauté the tofu until lightly browned. Remove the tofu and sauté the onion, celery, and zucchini. (Add a little water or gravy if necessary.) Add the minced garlic, walnuts, and rice.

In another bowl, combine the egg and extra yolk, vinegar, tamari, lemon juice, and ginger.

Preheat oven to 375°F. Line 12 muffin wells with foil baking cups.

Add the rice polish or flour and sesame seeds to the tofu mixture. Fill the muffin cups and garnish each with the nuts. Bake for 18 to 20 minutes.

Yield: 12 muffins.

Approximately 120 calories each.

5
GO ANYWHERE
FRUIT 'N' NUT MUFFINS

Right now there's snow on the ground, but I can go to my freezer for muffins made from the luscious peaches we picked last summer. Blueberries, too, that we picked in August are nestled in muffins stored in our freezer and brighten our Sunday brunches with the taste of summer's bounty. Every mouthful of these muffins is crunchy with nuts and deliciously moist with flavorful fruit. As one of my grandchildren remarked, "They make music in my mouth!"

I use fruit in muffins not only for the marvelous flavor and texture it adds but also because of its vitamin and mineral content, which has a refreshing and restorative effect. For example, fruit is an excellent source of pectin, which helps to usher toxic chemicals out of the body.

Nuts are perfect companions for fruits, providing complementary amino acids, thus enriching the protein value of the muffins. Nuts also provide B vitamins, important minerals, and the essential fatty acids that have been shown to lower cholesterol levels and strengthen the immune system.

Cherry Almond Amaretto Muffins

Make these for very special occasions—they delight the eye and the palate. If you are a teetotaler, you can still enjoy these muffins. The alcohol evaporates in the heat, leaving the lovely Amaretto flavor in every luscious morsel.

½ cup chopped pitted Bing
    cherries
¼ cup Amaretto liqueur
2 eggs
2 tablespoons olive or vegetable
    oil
3 tablespoons honey
¼ teaspoon almond extract
¾ cup apple-raspberry or other
    fruit juice
2 tablespoons Amaretto liqueur

1½ cups sifted whole wheat
    pastry flour
2 tablespoons wheat germ
2 tablespoons oat bran
2 tablespoons lecithin granules
1 teaspoon baking powder
1 teaspoon baking soda
½ cup chopped almonds
    sliced almonds and cherry
    halves for garnish

In a small bowl, combine the cherries and Amaretto. Set aside. In a mixing bowl or food processor, blend the eggs, oil, honey, almond extract, fruit juice, and two tablespoons of additional Amaretto. Stir in the cherry mixture.

In another bowl, combine the pastry flour, wheat germ, oat bran, lecithin granules, baking powder, and baking soda.

Preheat oven to 400°F. Grease 12 average-size muffin cups with a lecithin and oil mixture or line with paper or foil cups.

Add the dry ingredients to the cherry mixture and blend just enough to moisten the pastry flour mixture. Stir in the chopped

almonds. Spoon the mixture into muffin cups and top with sliced almonds and a piece of cherry. Bake for 20 minutes.
Yield: 12 muffins.
Approximately 175 calories each.

Banana Maple Walnut Muffins

Moist, tender, and full of flavor, these potassium-rich muffins are a favorite with our children. Be sure to use very ripe bananas, the kind that just won't last until tomorrow.

¼ *cup wheat bran*
¼ *cup yogurt*
2 *eggs*
2 *tablespoons vegetable or olive oil*
3 *tablespoons maple syrup*
1 *cup mashed bananas (about 3 medium)*
1 *tablespoon lemon juice*
½ *cup plumped raisins*
1 *cup sifted whole wheat pastry flour*

½ *cup wheat germ*
½ *teaspoon baking powder*
½ *teaspoon baking soda*
1 *teaspoon ground cinnamon*
1 *teaspoon grated orange rind (optional)*
½ *cup chopped walnuts nuts or sunflower seeds for garnish*

In a small bowl, mix together the yogurt and bran. Set aside.
In a mixing bowl or food processor, blend together the eggs, oil, maple syrup, mashed bananas, and lemon juice. Add the yogurt-bran mixture and the raisins.

In another bowl, mix together the pastry flour, wheat germ, baking powder, baking soda, cinnamon, and orange rind.

Preheat oven to 375°F. Grease 12 regular-size muffin cups or 36 minimuffin cups with a lecithin and oil mixture or line with foil baking cups.

Add the dry ingredients to the banana mixture and process briefly—only until no pastry flour is visible. Stir in the nuts.

Spoon the batter into the prepared muffin cups. Top each with a piece of nut or a few sunflower seeds. Bake for 20 minutes or until tinged with a golden glow.

Yield: 12 regular-size muffins or 36 minimuffins.

Approximately 150 calories each for regular-size muffins, approximately 50 calories each for minimuffins.

Apricot Almond Muffins

A marvelous muffin—good-looking, good-tasting, and richly endowed with so many important nutrients. Almonds contribute protein, potassium, iron, calcium, and polyunsaturated fatty acids. They are an excellent complement to raisins and apricots, which provide vitamin A and iron.

12 almonds
12 dried apricots
 3 tablespoons honey
 2 eggs
 2 tablespoons olive or vegetable
     oil
⅔ cup buttermilk or yogurt
 1 teaspoon vanilla
 1 cup sifted whole wheat
     pastry flour

 1 cup rolled oats
 2 tablespoons oat bran
 2 teaspoons baking powder
 1 teaspoon baking soda
½ cup dried apricots, finely
     chopped
⅓ cup raisins, plumped

Soak the almonds and apricots overnight in enough water to cover them. Purée the almonds and apricots with their liquid in a food processor, then add and blend the honey, eggs, oil, buttermilk or yogurt, and vanilla.

In another bowl, mix together the pastry flour, oats, oat bran, baking powder, and baking soda.

Preheat oven to 400°F. Line 12 regular-size muffin wells with paper or foil baking cups, or grease with a mixture of lecithin and oil.

Combine the wet and dry mixtures and stir only until the dry ingredients are moistened. Fold in the apricots and raisins.

Spoon the batter into the muffin cups and bake for 15 to 20 minutes or until a cake tester comes out clean.
Yield: 12 large muffins.
Approximately 153 calories each.

Plum and Peanut Muffins

Preserve the flavor of juicy summer plums in these moist, crunchy muffins that provide lots of protein, calcium, potassium, and vitamin A.

½ cup chopped plums
½ cup apple or apple-apricot juice
2 eggs
2 tablespoons olive or vegetable oil
2 tablespoons honey
2 tablespoons molasses
1 cup sifted whole wheat flour

2 tablespoons wheat germ
2 tablespoons wheat bran
2 tablespoons oat bran
2 tablespoons soy granules or TVP (textured vegetable protein)
1 teaspoon baking powder
1 teaspoon baking soda
½ cup chopped peanuts

Add the plums to the juice to soak for about 15 minutes. In a mixing bowl or food processor, blend the eggs, oil, honey, molasses, and plums together with the juice in which they were soaked.

In another bowl, blend together the flour, wheat germ, wheat bran, oat bran, soy granules or TVP, baking powder, and baking soda.

Preheat oven to 400°F. Line 12 regular-size muffin wells with foil or paper liners, or grease with a mixture of lecithin and oil.

Combine the wet and dry mixtures and blend briefly, only until the ingredients are well combined. Stir in the peanuts. Spoon the batter into the muffin wells and bake for about 20 minutes or until a cake tester comes out clean.

Yield: 12 muffins.

Approximately 110 calories each.

Papaya Pumpkin Seed Muffins

Pumpkin seeds are rich in zinc, a mineral essential to growth, to healing, to strong bones, and to the male prostate gland. Pumpkin seeds also contribute protein and crunch to these sweet papaya muffins.

½ cup dried papaya, diced
¾ cup apple or apple-apricot
    juice
2 medium-size eggs
2 tablespoons olive or walnut
    oil
2 tablespoons molasses
1 tablespoon honey
2 tablespoons wheat bran
1 cup sifted whole wheat
    pastry flour

2 tablespoons wheat germ
½ teaspoon baking soda
1 teaspoon baking powder
1 teaspoon cinnamon
⅛ teaspoon nutmeg
    pinch of ginger
⅓ cup toasted pumpkin seeds
    pumpkin seeds for garnish

Soak the papaya in the apple juice for an hour, or overnight.

In a mixing bowl or food processor, blend together the eggs, oil, molasses, honey, wheat bran, and the juice in which the papaya was soaked.

In another bowl, mix together the pastry flour, wheat germ, baking soda, baking powder, and spices.

Preheat oven to 400°F. Line 12 muffin wells with paper or foil baking cups, or grease with a mixture of lecithin and oil.

Mix together the wet and dry ingredients only until the ingredients are well combined. Stir in the papaya and the pumpkin seeds. Spoon the batter into the muffin wells. Top each muffin with a few pumpkin seeds. Bake for 12 to 15 minutes or until a cake tester comes out clean.

Yield: 12 muffins.

Approximately 117 calories each.

Fuzzy Navel Peach Muffins

The flavors of orange and peaches team up in these delicate, fruity muffins that have a sweet surprise inside: orange marmalade. Peaches are a marvelous source of vitamin A, providing 21,000 I.U. in a single peach. They're also a perfect complement for the flavor and vitamin C provided by the oranges.

1 large or 2 medium-size
    peaches, cut up (about 1
    cup)
¾ cup orange juice
1 tablespoon honey
⅛ teaspoon almond extract
2 eggs
3 tablespoons olive or vegetable
    oil
1 cup sifted whole wheat
    pastry flour
1 teaspoon baking powder

1 teaspoon baking soda
2 tablespoons wheat germ
2 tablespoons oat bran
2 tablespoons soy flour
1 teaspoon cinnamon
    pinch of ground gloves
    few gratings of nutmeg or
       pinch ground nutmeg
4 tablespoons unsweetened
    orange marmalade (Sorrell
    Ridge is a good brand)
    chopped pecans for garnish

In a saucepan, combine the peaches, orange juice, honey, and almond extract and cook for about 10 minutes. Set aside to cool.

In a mixing bowl or food processor, blend together the eggs and oil. Stir in the cooled peach mixture.

In another bowl, mix together the pastry flour, baking powder, baking soda, wheat germ, oat bran, soy flour, cinnamon, cloves, and nutmeg.

Preheat oven to 400°F. Line 12 muffin cups with paper or foil baking cups, or grease with a mixture of lecithin and oil.

Add the pastry flour mixture to the peach mixture and mix gently just until the ingredients are well combined.

Fill each muffin cup about half full, then drop 1 teaspoon of orange marmalade in the center of each. Cover the marmalade with the remaining batter. Sprinkle the tops with chopped pecans. Bake for 20 to 25 minutes or until lightly browned on top and dry inside when pierced with a food pick or cake tester.

Yield: 12 muffins.

Approximately 128 calories each.

Apple Pecan Bran Muffins

Apples contribute pectin and crunchy moistness to these hearty muffins. Bran provides lots of fiber, which protects against bowel diseases and decreases absorption of cholesterol, thus reducing the incidence of cardiovascular disease. For added sweetness, toast these muffins and serve with apple butter.

2 large eggs
2 tablespoons olive or vegetable oil
1 cup buttermilk or yogurt
3 tablespoons molasses
2 tablespoons honey or barley malt
⅓ cup wheat bran
1½ cups sifted whole wheat pastry flour
½ cup rolled oats
2 teaspoons baking powder
1 teaspoon baking soda
2 teaspoons cinnamon
¼ teaspoon ginger
¼ teaspoon nutmeg
1 apple, chopped
½ cup chopped pecans

In a mixing bowl or food processor, blend together the eggs, oil, buttermilk or yogurt, molasses, and honey or barley malt. Stir in the wheat bran.

In another bowl, mix together the pastry flour, oats, baking powder, baking soda, cinnamon, ginger, and nutmeg.

Preheat oven to 400°F. Grease 12 regular-size muffin wells with a lecithin and oil mixture or line with baking cups.

Combine the 2 mixtures and mix briefly just until the ingredients are well blended. Then stir in the apple and pecans.

Spoon the batter into the muffin cups and bake for 20 to 25 minutes or until a cake tester comes out clean.
Yield: 12 muffins.
Approximately 146 calories each.

Blueberry Sunflower Muffins

Blueberries and muffins go together like love and marriage. Blueberries are rich in manganese, a mineral essential to healthy ligaments, and believe it or not, to mother love! (Animals deficient in manganese refuse to nurture their young.) If you use frozen berries, add another ¼ cup flour.

2 eggs
¼ cup honey
2 tablespoons softened
    unsalted butter, or olive
    or vegetable oil
½ cup buttermilk or yogurt
1 teaspoon vanilla
1 cup sifted whole wheat
    pastry flour

2 tablespoons wheat germ
2 tablespoons oat bran
1 teaspoon baking powder
1 teaspoon baking soda
1½ cups blueberries
½ cup sunflower seeds

In a mixing bowl or food processor, combine the eggs, honey, oil or butter, buttermilk or yogurt, and vanilla. In another bowl, combine the pastry flour, wheat germ, oat bran, baking powder, and baking soda. Stir in the blueberries.

Preheat oven to 350°F. Grease 12 regular-size muffin cups with a lecithin and oil mixture, or line with foil or paper baking cups.

Combine the two mixtures. Stir in the sunflower seeds. Spoon the batter into the muffin cups and bake for 20 minutes.

Yield: 12 muffins.

Approximately 146 calories each.

Banana Muffins with Hazelnut Topping

These high-potassium, high-energy treats are great for lunch boxes, for afternoon tea, or for breakfast or brunch. Spread with a blend of cottage cheese and peach or banana.

2 eggs
2 bananas (about ¾ cup)
3 tablespoons honey or
    molasses
2 tablespoons olive or vegetable
    oil
½ cup yogurt, buttermilk, or
    soured milk
1¼ cups sifted whole wheat
    pastry flour

2 tablespoons oat bran
2 tablespoons wheat germ
2 tablespoons wheat bran
½ teaspoon cinnamon
1 teaspoon baking powder
1 teaspoon baking soda
    chopped hazelnuts

In a mixing bowl or food processor, blend together the eggs, bananas, honey or molasses, oil, and yogurt, buttermilk, or soured milk.

In another bowl, mix together the pastry flour, oat bran, wheat germ, wheat bran, cinnamon, baking powder, and baking soda.

Preheat oven to 400°F. Grease the bottoms of 12 regular-size muffin pan cups with a mixture of lecithin and oil or line them with paper baking cups.

Combine the dry ingredients with the banana mixture and mix briefly, only until no flour is visible. Spoon the batter into the muffin cups. Top each muffin with chopped hazelnuts. Bake for 20 to 22 minutes or until the tops are golden. Cool for 5 minutes, then remove to a wire rack.

Yield: 12 muffins.

Approximately 120 calories each.

6

VERY SKINNY
SMART MUFFINS

All of the muffins in this book provide fewer calories than their commercial counterparts because they are low in fat and sweeteners. In this chapter, we've trimmed the calories even further, but without reducing the nutritional value. We do this by using vitamin- and mineral-rich foods that are low in calories, such as zucchini, wheat sprouts, tofu, peaches, and popcorn flour.

Cutting calories doesn't mean sacrificing taste, texture, and the joy of eating. The Heavenly Cheesecake Muffins taste like a zillion calories but have only 22. That's less than you imbibe when you eat a quarter of an apple!

The 15-calorie popcorn nosh is reminiscent of the stuff you gobbled up as a kid to get to the prize at the bottom of the box.

The prize you get with these Very Skinny Smart Muffins is much more gratifying—good-tasting treats and a figure fit for a bikini.

Zucchini Kugel Muffins

These muffins double as a side dish and as dessert. Zucchini provides vitamin A, calcium, some vitamin C and a smattering of the B family, fiber, and very few calories.

3 cups grated zucchini, drained	2 tablespoons wheat germ
	2 tablespoons oat bran
1 tablespoon honey	2 tablespoons lecithin granules
3 eggs	½ cup raisins, plumped
1 teaspoon cinnamon	½ cup chopped walnuts

Preheat oven to 350°F. Line 12 muffin wells with foil baking cups or grease with a mixture of lecithin and oil.

In a mixing bowl or food processor, mix together the zucchini, honey, and eggs. Add the cinnamon, wheat germ, oat bran, lecithin granules, raisins, and walnuts.

Spoon the batter into the muffin cups and bake for 20 minutes or until nicely browned.

Yield: 12 muffins.

Approximately 85 calories each.

Peachy Pecan Muffins

I make these muffins when peaches are ripe and plentiful, then store some in the freezer to enjoy in the middle of winter. They're great for an evening of playing Trivial Pursuit.

1 egg
2 tablespoons vegetable or
  olive oil
2 tablespoons honey
1 cup peach purée (1 large
  ripe peach whizzed in
  the food processor)
½ cup yogurt
½ cup rolled oats, uncooked
1¼ cups whole wheat pastry
  flour
2 tablespoons wheat germ

2 tablespoons oat bran
2 tablespoons wheat bran
1 tablespoon grated orange
  peel
2 teaspoons baking powder
1 teaspoon baking soda
1 cup chopped peaches
  peach conserve (Sorrell
  Ridge is a good
  brand—only 14 calories)
chopped pecans

In a mixing bowl or food processor, blend together the egg, oil, honey, peach purée, and yogurt.

In another bowl, mix together the oats, pastry flour, wheat germ, brans, orange peel, baking powder, and baking soda.

Preheat oven to 400°F. Line 12 regular-size muffin wells with paper baking cups or grease with a mixture of lecithin and oil.

Combine the dry ingredients and the peach mixture, stirring just until blended. Stir in the chopped peaches.

Spoon the batter into the muffin cups. Top each muffin with about ½ teaspoon of conserve if you are using it, then top each with a sprinkle of pecans. Bake for 20 to 25 minutes or until a cake tester comes out clean.

Yield: 12 muffins.

Approximately 94 calories each, without the topping; approximately 101 calories each, with peach conserve; approximately 106 calories each, with chopped almonds and conserve.

Tofu Cashew Cheeseless Cheesecake Muffins

This is a high-protein, low-calorie nosh that tastes deliciously fattening. These muffins have a creamy consistency that improves with age. Keep refrigerated and serve cold.

¼ cup raisins
¼ cup apple or apple-apricot juice
2 tablespoons tahini
1 teaspoon vanilla
1 tablespoon grated orange rind

2 tablespoons honey
1 tablespoon lemon juice
1 pound tofu, cubed
6 tablespoons popcorn flour cashew nuts

Soak the raisins in the juice for an hour or overnight.

In a food processor or blender, mix together the soaked raisins with the apple juice, tahini, vanilla, orange rind, honey, lemon juice, and tofu. Process until smooth.

Preheat oven to 350°F. Line 3 dozen minimuffin wells with foil or paper baking cups.

Put ½ teaspoon of popcorn flour in the bottom of each muffin cup, then spoon the batter on top of the flour. Place ½ cashew nut on top of each. Bake for 15 to 20 minutes.

Yield: 3 dozen minimuffins.

Approximately 22 calories each.

Popcorn Carob Cheesecake Muffins

Freeze these minimuffins, savor them slowly like an ice cream cone, and enjoy a nutritious sweet your waistline will love—only 33 calories each, including topping! Substitute 1 teaspoon vanilla-flavored whipped cream for the tofu topping, if you like, for the same calorie count.

1 egg
1 tablespoon honey
½ cup orange concentrate
1 teaspoon vanilla
½ cup cottage cheese
½ cup plumped raisins
1 cup popcorn flour*

¼ cup carob powder
2 tablespoons whole wheat
*   pastry flour*
2 teaspoons baking powder
½ teaspoon baking soda
1 teaspoon cinnamon

In a mixing bowl or food processor, blend the egg, honey, orange concentrate, vanilla, and cottage cheese. Stir in the raisins.

In another bowl, combine the popcorn flour, carob powder, whole wheat pastry flour, baking powder, baking soda, and cinnamon.

Line 24 minimuffin wells with paper liners. Preheat oven to 350°F.

Combine the two mixtures and mix briefly only to blend the ingredients.

Spoon the mixture into the muffin cups and bake for 15 minutes. Cool in pans for 10 minutes, then remove to a rack. When cool, top with maple tofu whip.

TOPPING

½ cup tofu
2 tablespoons maple syrup
1 tablespoon orange
   concentrate

1 tablespoon Kahlúa (optional)
1 tablespoon instant decaffein-
   ated coffee crystals

To make the topping, blend together in a food processor or blender the tofu, maple syrup, orange concentrate, Kahlúa, and coffee.

When cool, frost the muffins. Place the frosted muffins on a tray and freeze. Serve them directly from the freezer.

Yield: 2 dozen minimuffins.

Approximately 33 calories each.

*1½ cups of popcorn whizzed in a coffee mill or seed grinder yield 1 cup of popcorn flour. Blenders and food processors do not grind the popcorn fine enough.

The 15-Calorie Popcorn Nosh

Popcorn is high in fiber and very low in calories—the perfect solution for a snack attack. These maple-flavored popcorn balls also satisfy your sweet tooth.

2 tablespoons maple syrup   ¼ cup water
1 teaspoon vanilla   2½ cups popped corn

Combine the maple syrup, vanilla, and water in a small saucepan. Bring to a boil, then simmer for a few minutes. Pour this solution over the popcorn.

Line 6 regular-size muffin wells with paper baking liners. Preheat oven to 300°F.

Form the popcorn into fist-size balls and place in the muffin cups. Bake for 10 minutes.

Yield: 6 popcorn balls.

Approximately 15 calories each.

Heavenly Cheesecake Muffins

Indulge your yen for cheesecake without guilt. Each muffin has only 22 calories. You could add a dollop of unsweetened fruit conserve without endangering your waistline. Sorrell Ridge brand contains only 14 calories in a whole teaspoon.

8 ounces (1 cup) cottage
   cheese
2 eggs, separated
2 tablespoons whole wheat
   pastry flour

½ teaspoon vanilla
1 teaspoon lemon juice
1 teaspoon grated lemon rind
1 tablespoon honey

In a food processor, blend the cottage cheese until it is as smooth as cream. Add the egg yolks, pastry flour, vanilla, lemon juice, lemon rind, and honey and blend.

In another bowl, beat the egg whites until they stand in peaks.

Preheat oven to 300°F. Grease 24 minimuffin wells with a mixture of lecithin and oil or line with minimuffin paper baking cups.

Fold the egg whites into the cottage cheese mixture. Spoon the batter into the muffin wells and bake for 20 minutes.

Yield: 2 dozen minimuffins.

Approximately 22 calories each.

Light and Fluffy Cornmeal Muffins

Low-calorie popcorn flour adds flavor and a deliciously fluffy texture to these quick and easy muffins. Popcorn flour provides fiber, protein, and iron and is ridiculousy low in calories.

¼ cup sour cream
¾ cup milk
⅓ cup maple syrup or ¼ cup honey
2 eggs
¾ cup whole wheat pastry flour

1½ cups popcorn flour*
2 tablespoons oat bran
2 tablespoons wheat germ
½ teaspoon baking soda
sesame seeds

Preheat oven to 400°F. Grease 12 regular-size muffin wells with a lecithin and oil mixture, or line with paper or foil cups.

In a bowl or food processor, combine the sour cream, milk, maple syrup or honey, and eggs. Process to combine.

In another bowl, mix together the flours, oat bran, wheat germ, and baking soda. Combine the two mixtures and blend only until no flour is visible. Spoon into the prepared muffin cups. Top with sesame seeds. Bake for 15 minutes.

Yield: 12 muffins.

Approximately 85 calories each.

*1½ cups of popcorn whizzed in a coffee mill or seed grinder yield 1 cup of popcorn flour. Blenders and food processors do not grind the popcorn fine enough.

7

BLESS-YOUR-HEART
MUFFINS

All the recipes in this book are extremely low in cholesterol. The recipes in this chapter, however, are loaded with ingredients that have been shown actually to *lower* cholesterol:

- Oat bran, according to nutritionist Jeffrey Bland, Ph.D., "is the best fiber supplement available for both lowering blood cholesterol and improving the management of blood sugar."
- Fruits, vegetables, whole grains, and legumes all have a beneficial effect on lowering blood cholesterol.
- Olive oil has been shown to lower the LDL (low-density lipoproteins) that are damaging to the arteries, without lowering the HDL (high-density lipoproteins) that are protective of the arteries. And in some instances olive oil actually increases HDL.
- Lecithin is a natural emulsifier that not only helps to keep your blood's cholesterol flowing freely, thus minimizing its tendency to form clots, but also has been shown in a recent study (at the Israel institute of Technology in Haifa) to lower LDL and increase HDL significantly. Lecithin was also shown to decrease triglyceride levels and to *inhibit platelet aggregation*. The optimal amount of lecithin supplementation ranges from 6 to 12 grams a day, according to the study.

Molasses is used as a sweetener in most of these muffins because of its high calcium and magnesium content. Both minerals are essential to the steady beat of your heart.

Spicy Bean Muffins

You won't believe how delicious a bean muffin can be! Beans are high in protein, low in calories, high in fiber, and contain no cholesterol. Pectin in the apple lowers cholesterol levels, and so does the oat bran. So enjoy in good health.

1 cup cooked, mashed pinto
   beans*
2 egg whites
3 tablespoons olive oil
1 teaspoon vanilla
2 tablespoons molasses or
   honey
½ cup sifted whole wheat
   pastry flour minus 2
   tablespoons

4 tablespoons oat bran
2 tablespoons lecithin granules
½ teaspoon baking soda
½ teaspoon ground cinnamon
⅛ teaspoon ground nutmeg
⅛ teaspoon ground cloves
1 cup diced apples
½ cup raisins
¼ cup chopped nuts

In a mixing bowl or food processor, combine the beans, egg whites, oil, vanilla, and molasses or honey.

In another bowl, combine the pastry flour, oat bran, lecithin granules, baking soda, and spices.

Preheat the oven to 350°F. Grease 12 regular-size muffin wells with a lecithin and oil mixture, or line with paper or foil cups.

Add the dry ingredients to the bean mixture and mix briefly to combine the ingredients. Stir in the apples, raisins, and nuts.

*1 cup of dried pinto beans will yield 2 cups cooked. The beans can be mashed with a little of the cooking water in your blender or food processor.

Spoon the batter into the muffin wells and bake for 20 minutes.
Yield: 12 muffins.
Approximately 110 calories each.

Blueberry Buttermilk Muffins

It's amazing that anything so good for you can taste so delicious. Blueberries provide vitamins A and C, potassium, calcium, iron, and manganese. The buttermilk (or yogurt) provides an acid medium that helps the body metabolize minerals. If you use frozen berries, add them in their frozen state to the dry ingredients, or the batter will turn blue.

2 egg whites, slightly beaten	1 tablespoon cinnamon
1/3 cup molasses	1 tablespoon grated orange rind
1 tablespoon olive oil	1 teaspoon baking soda
3/4 cup buttermilk or low-fat yogurt	1 teaspoon baking powder
1 cup sifted whole wheat pastry flour	1 1/2 cups blueberries
1/2 cup oat bran	walnuts and unsweetened blueberry conserve for garnish (Sorrell Ridge is a good brand)
3 tablespoons lecithin granules	
2 tablespoons wheat germ	

In a mixing bowl or food processor, blend together the egg whites, molasses, olive oil, and buttermilk or yogurt.

In another bowl, mix together the pastry flour, oat bran, lecithin granules, wheat germ, cinnamon, orange rind, baking soda, and baking powder.

Preheat oven to 400°F. Grease 12 regular-size muffin cups with a lecithin and oil mixture, or line with paper or foil baking cups.

Combine the 2 mixtures and mix just to moisten all the ingredients. Fold in the blueberries.

Spoon the batter into the muffin cups. Top each with ½ walnut and a dab of blueberry conserve. Bake for 15 to 20 minutes.

Yield: 12 muffins.

Approximately 125 calories each.

No-Egg Bran Apple Muffins

Here's a special treat for cholesterol-watchers. These eggless muffins are loaded with fiber, which has been shown to further lower cholesterol levels.

½ cup yogurt
½ cup wheat bran
1 cup whole wheat pastry flour
¼ cup wheat germ
¼ cup oat bran
½ cup rolled oats
2 teaspoons baking powder
1 teaspoon baking soda
½ teaspoon cinnamon

2 teaspoons grated orange rind
2 tablespoons oil
2 tablespoons molasses
2 large apples, shredded (2 cups)
½ cup raisins, plumped
½ cup sunflower seeds
walnuts or pecans as garnish

In a measuring cup or small bowl, combine the yogurt and wheat bran. Set aside. In a bowl, combine the pastry flour, wheat germ, oat bran, oats, baking powder, baking soda, cinnamon, and orange rind. Set aside.

In another bowl or food processor, combine the oil, molasses, shredded apples, plumped raisins, and the yogurt-wheat bran mixture. Process to combine.

Add the combined dry ingredients and the sunflower seeds and process only until the ingredients are well combined. Spoon into muffin tins that have been greased with a mixture of lecithin and oil. Top each one with ½ walnut or ½ pecan. Bake in preheated 350°F oven for about 25 to 30 minutes.

Yield: 12 large muffins.
Approximately 168 calories each.

Fruit 'n' Nut Oat Bran Muffins

Not only do these muffins contain no cholesterol and no concentrated sweetener, they also are rich in pectin, polyunsaturates, potassium, lecithin, and oat bran, which tend to lower cholesterol levels and enhance the health of the heart. As for your taste buds—they never had it so good.

1 apple, unpeeled, grated
1 cup raisins
1 cup chopped prunes
1 cup chopped walnuts
3 tablespoons oat bran
2 tablespoons lecithin granules
½ cup chopped almonds
3 egg whites, slightly beaten

In a mixing bowl, combine the apple, raisins, prunes, walnuts and almonds, oat bran, and lecithin granules. Add the egg whites, and mix to moisten the ingredients.

Preheat oven to 350°F. Line 3 dozen minimuffin cups with paper liners or grease with a mixture of lecithin and oil. Spoon the batter into the muffin cups and bake for 15 minutes.

Yield: 3 dozen minimuffins.

Approximately 55 calories each.

Sour Cream and Chive Muffins

The oat bran and lecithin in these muffins both tend to reduce cholesterol levels, making the sour cream in them more enjoyable. If you prefer, you can eliminate the sour cream and use 1 cup of yogurt. Serve them hot with yogurt creamless cheese.

½ cup sour cream
½ cup yogurt
1 clove garlic, minced
2 egg whites
2 tablespoons olive oil
1 tablespoon honey
1 cup sifted whole wheat pastry flour

2 tablespoons wheat germ
4 tablespoons oat bran
3 tablespoons lecithin granules
1 teaspoon baking powder
1 teaspoon baking soda
2 tablespoons chopped chives

In a small bowl, combine the sour cream, yogurt, and minced garlic. Set aside.

In a mixing bowl or food processor, mix together the egg whites, oil, honey, and sour cream mixture.

In another bowl, combine the pastry flour, wheat germ, oat bran, lecithin granules, baking powder, and baking soda.

Preheat oven to 400°F. Grease 12 regular-size muffin cups with an oil and lecithin mixture or line with foil baking cups.

Combine the wet and dry ingredients and mix only to combine (about 3 pulses of the food processor). Spoon the batter into the muffin cups, top with a sprinkle of chives, and bake for 20 minutes. **Yield:** 12 muffins.

Approximately 108 calories each when made with ½ cup of sour cream, approximately 95 calories each when made with 1 cup of yogurt and no sour cream.

8
LIFE-OF-THE-PARTY MUFFINS

These very special party muffins are for those occasions when you really want to impress your family and friends with your muffin *savoir-faire*.

Some of these muffins could double as cupcakes. In fact, we have put several of them together in a circle, put a candle in each one, and then sung "Happy Birthday" to a blushing child. The child then takes over and, instead of struggling with a knife and cake crumbs, distributes the muffins to the celebrants.

The more sophisticated muffins—those made with liqueurs, for instance—add a very merry note to the more adult celebrations. Far better to serve liqueurs in muffins than in a glass. You won't have to worry about driving skills being impaired—the alcohol evaporates in the baking process. The flavor remains. So enjoy!

Prune and Pistachio Muffins

Pistachios lend flavor, crunch, and elegance to these muffins, not to mention protein, iron, calcium, potassium, vitamin A, and a smattering of the vitamin B's—all at half the calorie cost of an equal amount of peanuts. Use the natural, undyed pistachios. Avoid those covered with red dye.

2 eggs	2 tablespoons wheat germ
3 tablespoons cream	2 tablespoons wheat bran
⅔ cup yogurt	2 teaspoons lemon rind
2 tablespoons softened butter or olive oil	1 teaspoon baking powder
4 tablespoons honey	1 teaspoon baking soda
1 cup diced prunes, plumped	⅓ cup chopped pistachios
1¾ cups sifted whole wheat pastry flour	12 pistachios for garnish

In a mixing bowl or food processor, blend together the eggs, cream, yogurt, butter or olive oil, and honey. Stir in the prunes.

In another bowl, mix together the pastry flour, wheat germ, wheat bran, lemon rind, baking powder, and baking soda.

Preheat oven to 400°F. Line 12 regular-size muffin wells with paper or foil baking cups, or grease with a mixture of lecithin and oil.

Combine the wet and dry mixtures and stir only until the dry ingredients are moistened. Fold in the chopped pistachios.

Spoon the batter into the muffin cups. Place a pistachio on top of each. Bake for 15 to 20 minutes or until a cake tester comes out clean. **Yield:** 12 muffins.

Approximately 148 calories each.

Mocha Kahlúa Cheesecake Muffins

These marvelous muffins are reminiscent of the cakes we enjoyed in Italy, where they have mastered the art of baking with liqueurs. They're perfect for dessert-and-coffee occasions at your house after a movie or the theater.

4 tablespoons cream cheese
2 tablespoons Kahlúa liqueur
2 tablespoons frozen orange
    concentrate
1 tablespoon honey
1 teaspoon vanilla
½ teaspoon cinnamon
2 eggs
¾ cup buttermilk
3 tablespoons vegetable or
    olive oil
3 tablespoons honey
1 tablespoon frozen orange
    concentrate

1 tablespoon instant coffee
    dissolved in 1 tablespoon
    boiling water
1 cup sifted whole wheat
    pastry flour
3 tablespoons carob powder
2 tablespoons wheat germ
1 teaspoon baking soda
1 teaspoon baking powder
½ cup raisins, plumped
½ cup chopped nuts or
    sunflower seeds
coconut and Bing cherries
    for garnish

In a small bowl or food processor, blend together the cream cheese, Kahlúa, orange concentrate, honey, vanilla, and cinnamon. Refrigerate.

In a large bowl or food processor, blend together the eggs, buttermilk, oil, honey, 1 tablespoon of orange concentrate, and 1 tablespoon of instant coffee dissolved in water. Combine this with the cheese mixture above.

In another bowl, mix together the pastry flour, carob powder, wheat germ, baking soda, and baking powder.

Preheat oven to 375°F. Grease 12 regular-size muffin cups with a mixture of lecithin and oil, or line with paper or foil baking cups. Combine the wet and dry ingredients. Stir in the raisins and nuts or sunflower seeds. Spoon mixture into muffin cups and garnish with coconut or Bing cherries.

Bake for 20 to 25 minutes or until a cake tester comes out clean. Let the muffins rest for 5 minutes, then remove to a rack to cool. When the muffins are cool, frost with the cream cheese–Kahlúa icing. **Yield:** 12 muffins.

Approximately 171 calories each.

Jack-o'-Lantern Muffins

Make these tasty muffins for Halloween and the kids will stay home! The pumpkin (a member of the squash family) provides calcium, phosphorus, potassium, iron, and a whopping 15,000 I.U. of vitamin A in every cup. Vitamin A improves your vision, keeps your skin healthy-looking, and increases your resistance to infection.

2 eggs
3 tablespoons honey
3 tablespoons olive or vegetable oil
1 tablespoon molasses
1 cup mashed pumpkin
1 cup sifted whole wheat pastry flour
2 tablespoons wheat germ
2 tablespoons oat bran

1 teaspoon baking powder
1 teaspoon baking soda
2 teaspoons cinnamon
¼ teaspoon nutmeg
¼ teaspoon ground cloves
1 tablespoon grated orange rind
½ cup raisins, plumped coconut or chopped nuts

CHEESE TOPPING

½ cup cottage cheese	½ teaspoon vanilla
4 tablespoons cream cheese	½ teaspoon lemon juice
2 tablespoons honey	

To make the topping, blend together the cottage cheese, cream cheese, honey, vanilla, and lemon juice in a blender or food processor until smooth.

To make the muffins, blend together in a mixing bowl or food processor the eggs, honey, oil, molasses, and pumpkin.

In another bowl, mix together the pastry flour, wheat germ, oat bran, baking powder, baking soda, cinnamon, nutmeg, cloves, and orange rind. Stir in the raisins.

Preheat oven to 400°F. Line 12 regular-size muffin wells with paper baking cups or grease with a mixture of lecithin and oil.

Mix together the pumpkin mixture and the dry ingredients. Put a tablespoon of batter in each muffin cup, then add a teaspoon of the topping. Top with the remaining batter. Bake for 20 to 25 minutes or until a cake tester comes out clean. Cool on a wire rack, then frost each muffin with the remaining cheese topping and garnish with coconut or chopped nuts.

Yield: 12 muffins.

Approximately 118 calories each without topping, approximately 142 calories each with topping, approximately 147 if you add coconut or chopped nuts.

Carob Banana Boat Muffins

If your kids are hooked on chocolate, try these delightful muffins. Make them ahead of a school trip or birthday party and store them in the freezer. They taste best when they're cold. Carob has the taste of chocolate without the oxalic acid, theobromine, and fat. Carob is high in potassium and low in calories.

1 large egg or 2 small eggs
2 tablespoons softened butter
   or olive oil
3 tablespoons honey or
   molasses
¾ cup mashed bananas (2
   small)
⅔ cup yogurt or buttermilk
1 teaspoon vanilla
1¼ cups whole wheat pastry
   flour
⅓ cup carob powder

2 tablespoons wheat germ
2 tablespoons oat bran
2 tablespoons wheat bran
2 teaspoons baking powder
1 teaspoon baking soda
1 tablespoon grated orange
   rind
1 teaspoon cinnamon
½ cup raisins, plumped
   walnuts and carob chips for
   garnish

In a mixing bowl or food processor, blend together the egg or eggs, butter or olive oil, honey or molasses, bananas, yogurt or buttermilk, and vanilla.

In another bowl, mix together the pastry flour, carob powder, wheat germ, oat bran, wheat bran, baking powder, baking soda, orange rind, and cinnamon.

Preheat oven to 400°F. Line 12 regular-size muffin wells with paper or foil baking cups, or grease with a mixture of lecithin and oil.

Combine the wet and dry mixtures and mix briefly, only until the dry ingredients are moistened. Stir in the raisins.

Spoon the batter into the muffin wells. Place ¼ walnut in the center of each, then place the carob chips in a circle around the walnut. Bake for 18 to 20 minutes.

Yield: 12 muffins.

Approximately 143 calories each.

Carob Mint Cashew Muffins

A lovely dessert muffin with a refreshing, minty flavor. Carob, also known as St. John's bread, could be said to be worth its weight in gold. In ancient times the seed of the carob was used as a standard by which to measure a carat of gold.

2 eggs
3 tablespoons olive or vegetable oil
3 tablespoons honey
1 tablespoon molasses
1 cup creamy carob mint tea (divided)*
1 cup sifted whole wheat pastry flour

½ cup carob powder
1 teaspoon baking powder
½ teaspoon baking soda
½ cup chopped cashews or walnuts
6 whole cashew nuts

*Creamy carob mint tea is available in most gourmet and health-food stores.

CAROB MINT TOPPING

¼ *cup carob powder*	½ *cup creamy carob mint tea*
2 *tablespoons honey*	2 *drops peppermint extract*

To make the topping, combine the carob powder, honey, and tea in a small saucepan. Bring to a boil, stirring constantly. Boil slowly for about 5 minutes. Remove from the heat, cool, and add the peppermint extract.

To make the muffins, blend together the eggs, oil, honey, molasses, and tea in a mixing bowl or food processor.

In another bowl, mix together the pastry flour, carob powder, baking powder, and baking soda.

Preheat oven to 400°F. Line 12 regular-size muffin wells with paper baking cups or grease with a mixture of lecithin and oil.

Combine the wet and dry mixtures and mix briefly, just enough to moisten the ingredients. Stir in the chopped nuts. Spoon 1 tablespoon of batter into each muffin well. Place about ½ teaspoon of carob mint topping on each, then distribute the rest of the batter, filling the muffin wells about ⅔ full. Top each with ½ cashew nut. Bake for 15 to 18 minutes or until nicely rounded and a cake tester comes out clean. Cool on a rack. Then swirl the rest of the carob mint topping around the cashew.

Yield: 12 muffins.

Approximately 166 calories each.

9

SMART MUFFINS
FOR THE ALLERGIC

If any members of your family are allergic to cow's milk, wheat, corn, chocolate, or eggs, they can still enjoy muffins. The recipes in this chapter have been devised to bypass one or more of these common allergens.

In addition, you can adapt any recipe from the rest of the book by following these guidelines:

COW'S MILK

If you must avoid cow's milk, substitute herbal teas, fruit juice, or nut milk. Here are some recipes:

Peanut milk: Blend together ½ cup of shelled, skinned peanuts with 2 cups of water. Strain. The chunks that remain can be added to granola or baked goods, or eaten on the spot.

Almond milk: Blend one cup of almonds with 2 to 4 cups of water. Blend the nuts first with a small amount of water, then add more to desired thickness.

Sesame milk: Blend 1 cup of sesame seeds with 3 cups of water. Blend the seeds first with 1 cup of water. Add the remaining water until the desired consistency is achieved.

Wheat milk: Fill a thermos halfway with wheat seeds. Add hot water to within 1 inch of the top. Cork and leave overnight. The next morning, grind the soaked seeds in a blender.

CORN

If you're allergic to corn, make your own baking powder. Most commercial baking powders include cornstarch. Make your own baking powder by combining ¼ teaspoon of bicarbonate of soda with ½ teaspoon of cream of tartar. This is equivalent to 1 teaspoon of baking powder.

And don't lick stamps or envelopes. The adhesive may contain small quantities of corn. So does chewing gum, powdered sugar, dextrose, white vinegar, aspirin and other tablets, and many commercial canned products.

EGGS

If you're allergic to eggs, remember that egg substitutes contain egg whites and nonfat milk solids.

In baking, you can achieve the emulsifying effect of 1 egg by combining 2 tablespoons of whole wheat flour, ½ teaspoon of oil, ½ teaspoon of baking powder, and 2 tablespoons of milk, water, or fruit juice. Or substitute 1 mashed banana, 1 tablespoon of liquid lecithin, or 1 tablespoon of gelatin for the missing egg.

WHEAT

If you're allergic to wheat, consider these substitutions: For 1 cup of wheat flour, use:

1⅓ cups ground rolled oats; or	*½ cup barley flour; or*
⅝ cup rice flour plus ⅓ cup rye flour; or	*1¼ cups rye flour*

CHOCOLATE

If you're allergic to chocolate, not to worry. None of the recipes in this book contains chocolate.

If you wish to adapt other recipes that call for chocolate, substitute carob powder measure for measure. As a substitute for 1 square of chocolate, use 3 level tablespoons of carob powder plus 2 tablespoons of milk or water.

Dynamite Millet Raisin Muffins

Millet is one of the most nutritious and well balanced of all the grains. It is also the least allergic and is easy to digest. It is very high in protein, the vitamin B's, lecithin, and minerals. Its high mineral content makes it an alkaline food. Other grains have an acid reaction. Millet is considered an outstanding antacid food, well tolerated by ulcer and colitis patients.

1 cup raisins	2 tablespoons rice polish
¾ cup fruit juice or water	2 tablespoons soy flour
1 egg	2 teaspoons baking powder
1 cup buttermilk, yogurt, or sour milk	1 teaspoon baking soda
2 tablespoons honey	1 teaspoon cinnamon
1 tablespoon molasses	1 tablespoon grated orange rind
1 cup millet flour	pinch of ground cloves
1 cup uncooked rolled oats	pinch of ginger
2 tablespoons oat bran	½ cup sunflower seeds

In a saucepan, combine the raisins and fruit juice or water, bring to a boil, then simmer for 5 minutes. Set aside to cool.

In a mixing bowl or food processor, blend together the egg, buttermilk or yogurt, or sour milk, honey, and molasses.

In another bowl, mix together the flour, oats, oat bran, rice polish, soy flour, baking powder, baking soda, cinnamon, orange rind, cloves, and ginger.

Preheat oven to 400°F. Line 12 muffin wells with paper liners or grease with a mixture of lecithin and oil.

Add the cooled raisin mixture to the liquid ingredients, then add the dry ingredients and mix briefly only until the ingredients are well combined. Stir in the sunflower seeds.

Fill the muffin wells with the batter and bake for 25 minutes or until the tops are well rounded and golden and a cake tester or wooden pick inserted in the center comes out clean.

Yield: 12 muffins.

Approximately 115 calories each.

Buckwheat Pumpkin Spice Muffins

Use white buckwheat flour for a mild and mellow flavor. It's made from unroasted whole groats. These muffins are moist, tender, and flavorful if you don't overbake them. Buckwheat muffins tend to dry out quickly if cooked too long.

2 eggs
¾ cup mashed, cooked pumpkin
2 tablespoons olive or vegetable oil
⅔ cup milk or fruit juice
2 tablespoons honey
1 tablespoon molasses
1 cup buckwheat flour
¼ cup soy flour
1 tablespoon baking powder

1 teaspoon baking soda
1 teaspoon cinnamon
1 tablespoon grated orange rind
½ teaspoon ginger
¼ teaspoon ground cloves
⅛ teaspoon freshly grated nutmeg
½ cup raisins

In a mixing bowl or food processor, blend together the eggs, pumpkin, oil, milk or fruit juice, honey, and molasses.

In another bowl, mix together the flours, baking powder, baking soda, spices, and raisins.

Preheat oven to 400°F. Grease 12 regular-size muffin cups with a lecithin and oil mixture or line with foil baking cups. Bake for 15 to 20 minutes or until a cake tester comes out clean.

Yield: 12 muffins.

Approximately 113 calories each.

Rye, Rice, and Raisin Muffins

Crisp tops, a tender crumb, and a marvelous fragrance make these *wheat-free* muffins very popular, even among those who can handle wheat. The wheat polish in these muffins is an excellent source of the B vitamin niacin, which reduces blood cholesterol levels and contributes to mental and emotional health.

2 eggs	1 teaspoon baking powder
2 tablespoons molasses	½ teaspoon baking soda
1 tablespoon honey	1 tablespoon grated orange
2 tablespoons olive oil	rind
1 cup yogurt or buttermilk	1 teaspoon cinnamon
1¾ cups rye flour	¼ teaspoon ground cloves
¼ cup rice polish	¼ teaspoon ground nutmeg
3 tablespoons lecithin granules	½ cup raisins, plumped
3 tablespoons oat bran	½ cup sunflower seeds

In a mixing bowl or food processor, blend together the eggs, molasses, honey, olive oil, and yogurt or buttermilk.

In another bowl, mix together the rye flour, rice polish, lecithin granules, oat bran, baking powder, baking soda, orange rind, cinnamon, cloves, and nutmeg.

Preheat oven to 400°F. Line 12 regular-size muffin wells with paper or foil baking cups, or grease with lecithin and oil.

Combine the two mixtures, then stir in the raisins and seeds. Spoon the batter into the muffin wells and bake for 12 to 15 minutes or until a cake tester comes out clean.

Yield: 12 muffins.

Approximately 143 calories each.

Tofu Bran Blueberry Eggless Muffins

High-protein, high-fiber, low-calorie, no cholesterol—these muffins provide a nutritional bonanza especially valuable to those who cannot eat eggs. They're great as an afternoon pickup or late-night snack.

½ cup wheat bran
1 cup buttermilk, sour
  milk, or yogurt
½ cup drained, mashed tofu
2 tablespoons olive or vegetable
  oil
3 tablespoons honey
¾ cup applesauce
½ cup wheat sprouts (optional)
1 cup sifted whole wheat
  pastry flour
¼ cup oat bran

2 tablespoons lecithin granules
1 teaspoon baking soda
1 teaspoon baking powder
1 tablespoon grated orange
  rind
½ teaspoon cinnamon
  grating of whole nutmeg
¼ teaspoon allspice
1½ to 2 cups blueberries
½ cup sunflower seeds
  orange marmalade for
  garnish

In a small bowl, combine the wheat bran and buttermilk, sour milk, or yogurt. In another small bowl or food processor, blend together the tofu, oil, honey, and applesauce. Add the bran mixture and the wheat sprouts.

In another bowl, combine the pastry flour, oat bran, lecithin granules, baking soda, baking powder, orange rind, cinnamon, nutmeg, and allspice. Stir in the blueberries.

Preheat oven to 375°F. Grease 12 muffin wells with a lecithin and oil mixture, or line with foil or paper cups.

Combine the two mixtures gently, trying not to break the blueberries. Fold in the sunflower seeds.

Spoon the batter into the muffin wells, and top each with a dab of orange marmalade (Sorrell Ridge unsweetened or your own).

Bake for 25 minutes or until toasty brown and a toothpick inserted in the center comes out clean.

Yield: 12 large muffins.

Approximately 116 calories each.

Maple Pecan Rye and Millet Muffins

A very nice consistency, a tender crumb, and a lovely maple flavor. The rye flour in these delicious muffins provides body-building protein, high-energy complex carbohydrates, and a hearty flavor that marries well the mild flavor and high mineral content of the millet flour.

2 large eggs
3 tablespoons olive or vegetable oil
⅓ cup maple syrup
¾ cup orange or apple juice
1 cup millet flour

1 cup rye flour
1 teaspoon baking soda
1 teaspoon baking powder
½ cup chopped pecans or walnuts
pecans for garnish

In a mixing bowl or food processor, blend together the eggs, oil, maple syrup, and juice.

In another bowl, mix together the flours, baking soda, and baking powder.

Preheat oven to 400°F. Line 12 regular-size muffin wells with paper or foil baking cups, or grease with a mixture of lecithin and oil.

Combine the wet and dry ingredients and blend only until the ingredients are well blended. Stir in the chopped nuts.

Spoon the batter into the muffin wells. Top each with a pecan nugget and bake for 18 to 20 minutes or until a cake tester comes out clean.

Yield: 12 muffins.
Approximately 152 calories each.

Pumpernickel Currant Muffins

These muffins make music in your mouth and in your arteries. Currants are a good source of omega 3 and omega 6 fatty acids, both of which enhance your chances of avoiding a heart attack or stroke by reducing cholesterol and triglycerides. I developed these muffins for my granddaughter who is allergic to wheat, but everybody is gobbling them up!

2 eggs	1 teaspoon baking soda
3 tablespoons olive or vegetable oil	1 teaspoon baking powder
	½ teaspoon cinnamon
4 tablespoons molasses	¼ teaspoon cloves
1 cup yogurt	¼ teaspoon allspice
1 cup rye flour	1 tablespoon grated orange rind
¼ cup brown rice flour	
2 tablespoons carob powder	¾ cup currants
¼ cup cornmeal	½ cup roasted chopped filberts
2 tablespoons lecithin granules	filbert halves for garnish
2 tablespoons oat bran	

In a mixing bowl or food processor, blend together the eggs, oil, molasses, and yogurt.

In another bowl, combine the flours, carob powder, cornmeal, lecithin granules, oat bran, baking soda, baking powder, and the spices.

Preheat oven to 375°F. Line 12 regular-size muffin wells with baking cups or grease with a mixture of oil and lecithin.

Combine the wet and dry mixtures and mix briefly, just to combine. Stir in the currants and the chopped filberts. Spoon the mixture into the muffin wells, top each with a filbert, and bake for about 20 minutes.

Yield: 12 muffins.

Approximately 177 calories each.

Brown Rice Hazelnut Muffins

These three-flour muffins have amino acids that complement each other; thus they provide protein of high biological value. They are incredibly delicious when served with yogurt cheese and apple butter.

2 eggs
3 tablespoons olive or vegetable
   oil
3 tablespoons honey
1 teaspoon vanilla
⅔ cup buttermilk, yogurt, or
   sour milk
½ cup cooked brown rice
½ cup plumped raisins

2 tablespoons millet, soy, or
   rice flour
⅔ cup rye flour
½ cup chick-pea flour
2 teaspoons baking powder
1 teaspoon baking soda
½ teaspoon cinnamon
¼ teaspoon nutmeg
12 hazelnuts

In a mixing bowl or food processor, blend together the eggs, oil, honey, vanilla, and buttermilk, yogurt, or sour milk. Stir in the rice and the plumped and cooled raisins.

In another bowl, combine the flours, baking powder, baking soda, cinnamon, and nutmeg.

Preheat oven to 400°F. Line 12 regular-size muffin wells with baking cups or grease with a mixture of lecithin and oil.

Combine the wet and dry ingredients and stir only enough to moisten. Spoon the batter into the muffin wells, top each muffin with a hazelnut, and bake for 15 to 20 minutes or until the tops are brown and rounded and a cake tester comes out clean.

Yield: 12 muffins.

Approximately 146 calories each.

Raw Fruit Muffins

These are hypoallergenic dreams—*no wheat, no eggs, no dairy*—but what a lot of nutrition they deliver! Raw foods provide many important enzymes that are zapped by heat. The blend of nuts, seeds, and fruit provides iron, calcium, magnesium, and many valuable trace minerals that, in small amounts, play an essential role in the body.

½ cup pitted dates
½ cup dried figs
½ cup raisins
½ cup sunflower seeds
½ cup chopped almonds
¼ cup chopped pecans or
    walnuts
1 tablespoon grated orange
    rind
1 teaspoon grated lemon rind

½ cup unsweetened coconut
1 chopped apple
2 tablespoons honey
¼ cup orange juice
2 teaspoons lemon juice
2 tablespoons Amaretto,
    brandy, or apple juice
½ teaspoon cinnamon
½ teaspoon nutmeg
sesame seeds

Combine all the ingredients except the sesame seed in a blender or food processor. Line 24 minimuffin wells with paper liners. Form the batter into walnut-size balls, roll each one in sesame seeds, and place in the muffin cups. No need to bake these muffins—they're ready to eat, or can be stored in your freezer.

Yield: 24 minifruitcakes.

Approximately 86 calories each.

Steamed Raisin Muffins

When you don't want to use the oven, use a steamer and make these moist, puddinglike muffins. This recipe calls for rye flour, but you could substitute whatever kind meets your family's taste and allergy requirements. For the raisins, you could substitute currants, prunes, or apricots.

2 eggs	¼ cup wheat bran
2 tablespoons olive oil or melted butter	¼ cup oat bran
	2 teaspoons baking powder
2 tablespoons honey or molasses	1 teaspoon cinnamon
	1 tablespoon grated orange rind
½ cup milk or fruit juice	
½ cup rye flour	½ raisins

In a mixing bowl or food processor, blend the eggs, olive oil or butter, honey or molasses, and milk or fruit juice.

In another bowl, combine the flour, wheat and oat bran, baking powder, cinnamon, and orange rind.

Combine the wet and dry ingredients, then stir in the raisins. Spoon the batter into 6 buttered custard cups and let steam for 35 minutes. Very good with vanilla sauce (see the recipe on page 160).
Yield: 6 muffins.
Approximately 150 calories each.

10
EXOTIC MUFFINS

This chapter includes muffins that contain unorthodox ingredients you don't usually associate with muffins. They can be served for an infinite variety of occasions. They're wholesome, flavorful, and adapt well to fancy dessert tray, lunch box, or brown bag.

The Popovers, when stuffed with tuna or salmon salad, give pizzazz to an everyday dish. They can also be stuffed with ice cream, whipped cream, or custard for an elegant dessert.

The Pumpkin Peach Chutney Muffins have a character all their own, quite different form the usual muffin. You probably wouldn't want them for breakfast, but they do elevate a lunch or dinner to gourmet status.

The Happy New Year Honey Cake Muffins with Kahlúa or Amaretto get the new year going on a heady note, and you simply must try the Powerhouse Carrot Coconut Muffins. They've got so much going for them, they could meet the standards set by every category of muffin in this book.

Pumpkin Peach Chutney Muffins

These muffins have an appealing, spunky flavor. Serve them warm with yogurt cream cheese and additional chutney, a tangy, sweet-and-sour condiment made with fruits, nuts, and spices.

2 large eggs
2 tablespoons olive, walnut, or vegetable oil
2 tablespoons honey
½ cup buttermilk or yogurt
1 cup puréed pumpkin
2 tablespoons wheat bran
¾ cup peach chutney (see the following recipe)
1½ cups whole wheat pastry flour

2 tablespoons wheat germ
2 tablespoons oat bran
2 tablespoons lecithin granules
1 teaspoon baking soda
1 teaspoon baking powder
1½ teaspoons cinnamon
¼ teaspoon freshly grated nutmeg
⅛ teaspoon allspice
1 teaspoon grated orange rind

In a mixing bowl or food processor, blend together the eggs, oil, honey, buttermilk or yogurt, pumpkin, wheat bran, and chutney.

In another bowl, mix together the pastry flour, wheat germ, oat bran, lecithin granules, baking soda, baking powder, cinnamon, nutmeg, allspice, and orange rind.

Preheat oven to 400°F. Line 12 regular-size muffin wells with baking cups, or grease with a mixture of lecithin and oil.

Combine the wet and dry ingredients and stir the mixture until just combined. Spoon the batter into the muffin wells and bake for about 20 minutes or until a tester comes out clean.

Yield: 12 muffins.

Approximately 111 calories each.

Peach Chutney

1¼ cups sliced peaches
3 tablespoons honey
1½ tablespoons apple cider,
raspberry or wine vinegar
¾ teaspoon minced, peeled
ginger root or ½
teaspoon ground ginger

½ cup raw cashews, coarsely
chopped
½ cup raisins

In a small bowl, combine the peaches, honey, vinegar, and ginger and mix well. Stir in the cashews and raisins and mix again.
Yield: about 2¼ cups.
Approximately 25 calories in 1 tablespoon.
Variation: Use apricot, pear, or apple for the chutney.

Happy New Year Honey Cake Muffins

We serve these miniature honey cakes with sliced apples to symbolize our wish for a sweet and fruitful year. We use apricots, which are very rich in blood-building iron, and walnuts, a good source of omega 3 fatty acids, to help make it a year of good health.

4 large eggs
2 tablespoons olive oil,
 walnut oil, or vegetable
 oil
½ cup honey
½ cup fruit juice or herbal tea
3 tablespoons applesauce
2 tablespoons brandy, Kahlúa,
 or Amaretto liqueur
3 cups sifted whole wheat
 pastry flour
3 tablespoons lecithin granules
3 tablespoons oat bran
2 tablespoons wheat germ
3 tablespoons soy flour or
 powder

½ teaspoon allspice
1 teaspoon ground cloves
½ teaspoon cinnamon
1 teaspoon baking soda
1½ teaspoons baking powder
1 cup raisins
12 dried apricots, chopped or
 diced
½ cup chopped walnuts
 orange or orange cherry
 marmalade, unsweetened
 (Sorrell Ridge is good)
 sliced or chopped almonds
 for garnish

In a large mixing bowl or food processor, blend together the eggs, oil, honey, fruit juice or herbal tea, applesauce, and brandy or liqueur.

In another bowl, mix together the pastry flour, lecithin granules, oat bran, wheat germ, soy flour or powder, spices, baking soda, and baking powder.

Preheat oven to 350°F. Grease 18 regular-size muffin wells with a lecithin and oil mixture, or line with foil or paper cups.

Combine the wet and dry ingredients and mix only until well blended. Stir in the raisins, apricots, and walnuts. Half fill the muffin wells with batter. Spoon a teaspoon of conserve on each one, then divide the remaining batter among the muffins. Top each with a few almond slices or chopped almonds.

Bake for 20 to 25 minutes or until a cake tester comes out clean.
Yield: 18 muffins.
Approximately 190 calories each.

Powerhouse Carrot Coconut Muffins

These muffins are exceptionally high in protein, fiber, and beta carotene—shown to be an effective antioxidant that helps to hold back the aging process and retard the development of malignancies. You could make a meal out of one with a salad and be very well nourished.

¾ cup hot water
½ cup raisins
2 carrots, grated (about 1 cup)
2 large eggs
2 tablespoons molasses
1 tablespoon honey
2 tablespoons olive or vegetable oil
2 tablespoons wheat bran
1¼ cups sifted whole wheat pastry flour
¼ cup rice polish
3 tablespoons oat bran

¼ cup lecithin granules
¼ cup dry milk powder
3 tablespoons sesame seeds
1 tablespoon nutritional yeast
1 teaspoon kelp
1 teaspoon baking soda
2 teaspoons baking powder
1½ teaspoons cinnamon
¼ teaspoon ground nutmeg
¼ teaspoon allspice
1 tablespoon grated orange rind
½ cup chopped walnuts
¼ cup flaked coconut

In a small bowl, soak the raisins in the hot water. Set aside.

In a mixing bowl or food processor, grate the carrots and blend with the eggs, molasses, honey, and oil. Mix in the wheat bran, and the water the raisins were soaked in.

In another bowl, mix together the pastry flour, rice polish, oat bran, lecithin granules, milk powder, sesame seeds, nutritional yeast, kelp, baking soda, baking powder, cinnamon, nutmeg, allspice, and orange rind.

Preheat oven to 400°F. Line 12 regular-size muffin wells with baking cups or grease with a mixture of lecithin and oil.

Combine the wet and dry mixtures and mix just until the ingredients are combined. Fold in the raisins, walnuts, and coconut. Spoon into the muffin cups and bake for about 20 minutes or until a cake tester comes out dry.

Yield: 12 muffins.

Approximately 182 calories each.

Popovers

These are shiny, crisp containers for tuna or salmon salad, or for elegant lemon custard or Bavarian cream fillings.

3 eggs
1 cup milk
2 tablespoons olive or vegetable oil

¾ cup whole wheat pastry flour
2 tablespoons wheat germ
2 tablespoons oat bran
2 tablespoons soy flour

Preheat oven to 375°F.

In a medium-size mixing bowl, using an electric beater, beat the eggs until foamy. Continue to beat as you add the milk and oil, then the pastry flour combined with the wheat germ, oat bran, and soy flour.

Grease 12 regular-size muffin wells with a lecithin and oil mixture.

Spoon the batter into the muffin wells till they are about ⅔ full. Bake for 40 to 50 minutes until golden brown and puffed up like tennis balls.

Yield: 12 popovers.

Approximately 78 calories each.

Variation: Sprinkle grated cheese on 1 tablespoon of the batter in each muffin well, then top with the rest of the batter.

Whole Wheat Cinnamon Raisin English Muffins

Split these muffins with a fork and toast the cut sides. Serve with yogurt cheese and fruit conserve.

1 tablespoon dry yeast	3¼ cups whole wheat bread flour
¼ cup warm water	¼ cup wheat germ
1 teaspoon honey	1½ teaspoons cinnamon
1¾ cups warm milk	½ cup raisins

In a small bowl, dissolve the yeast in the water and add the honey. Set aside to proof for 10 minutes.

In a larger bowl, combine the milk, bread flour, wheat germ, and cinnamon. Add the yeast mixture and raisins and beat well.

Cover and let rise in a warm place until double in bulk (about 1 hour).

Heat a heavy griddle, skillet, or baking sheet on top of the stove. Brush with oil. Grease several crumpet rings, small tuna cans with both ends removed, or canning jar rings. Keep the heat under the griddle low.

With a spoon or ladle, half fill the rings. Cook the muffins about 6 minutes on each side or until brown on both sides.

Yield: 15 muffins.

Approximately 157 calories each.

11
SMART TOPPINGS FOR SMART MUFFINS

Toppings can add moistness and flavor to your muffins. In making your choice, consider these calorie counts:

Butter: 100 calories in 1 tablespoon
Sour cream: 475 calories per cup
Yogurt (whole milk): 152 calories per cup
Yogurt (partially skimmed milk): 123 calories per cup
Cream cheese: 100 calories per ounce
Cottage cheese (4.2 percent milk fat): 30 calories per ounce
Yogurt cream cheese (from whole milk yogurt): 40 calories per ounce
Yogurt cream cheese (made from partially skimmed milk yogurt): 38 calories per ounce
Tofu: 21½ calories per ounce

These toppings should be added on before baking: a sprinkling of rolled oats, poppy seeds, sunflower seeds, chopped peanuts, chopped almonds, almond slices, and walnut, pecan, and cashew halves.

The following toppings should be applied after the muffins are baked and cooled:

Yogurt Creamless Cheese

This spread has a pleasant tang and is low in calories.

Place 1 pint of plain yogurt in a colander lined with 3 layers of cheesecloth, a cheese bag, or a clean tea towel. Let it drain into a bowl for several hours or overnight. In the morning you will have 6 ounces of wonderful yogurt cheese. The liquid that has drained into the bowl is whey and can be used in soup or in baking.

The yogurt cheese can be spread plain on muffins or mixed with fruit conserve, nuts, spices, or flavorings.

Yield: 6 ounces.

Approximately 20 calories per tablespoon.

Apricot Almond Jam

½ cup dried apricots
6 whole almonds
½ cup raisins

apple juice to cover
1 teaspoon grated orange rind

Combine the apricots, almonds, and raisins in a jar. Cover with the apple juice. Let stand overnight in the refrigerator.

Whiz the soaked apricots, almonds, raisins, the residual apple juice, and the orange rind in a food processor or blender.

Yield: 1 cup.

Approximately 8½ calories in a teaspoon.

Vanilla Sauce

---

2 tablespoons butter
2 tablespoons whole wheat
    pastry flour

1 cup boiling water
2 tablespoons honey
1 teaspoon vanilla

In a saucepan, melt the butter, add the pastry flour, and stir until it bubbles. Add the boiling water and honey. Bring to a boil and cook for about 10 minutes. Add the vanilla.

Yield: about ⅔ cup.

Approximately 32 calories in a tablespoon.

Fig, Raisin, and Nut Spread

½ cup figs, diced
½ cup raisins
½ cup hazelnuts or skinned
    peanuts

1 tablespoon orange marma-
    lade, unsweetened

Combine the figs and raisins in a bowl or food processor, using a steel blade. Process to a smooth consistency. Add the nuts, and process until they are finely chopped. Stir in the orange marmalade. Spread on hot muffins.

If you have any of this spread left over, form into balls and roll in coconut or sesame seeds. Makes a delicious confection.

Yield: 1½ cups.

Approximately 12 calories in a teaspoon.

Banana Peanut Butter Delight

2 medium bananas
2–3 tablespoons honey or
   molasses

¼ cup yogurt
¼ teaspoon cinnamon
½ cup peanut butter

In a flat bowl or food processor, blend all the ingredients until smooth.

Yield: about 1 cup.

Approximately 22 calories in a teaspoon.

    This topping also makes delicious Popsicles. Just spoon into 3-ounce paper cups, insert Popsicle sticks, and freeze. Or top with crushed nuts and carob syrup to make darling little miniature sundaes. Let thaw a few minutes before slurping.

Banana Cottage Cheese Topping

A substantial topping that doubles as a dessert pudding.

½ cup cottage cheese
1 banana
½ teaspoon cinnamon

2 teaspoons unsweetened
   orange marmalade (Sor-
   rell Ridge)

In a flat bowl or food processor, blend all the ingredients together until smooth.

Yield: about ½ cup.

Approximately 17 calories in a tablespoon.

Peanut Butter Yogurt Topping

Try a teaspoon on a toasted muffin. Heavenly!

¼ cup peanut butter   *½ teaspoon cinnamon*
¼ cup yogurt

Blend all the ingredients in a mixing bowl or food processor.
Yield: ½ cup.
Approximately 8 calories in a teaspoon.

INDEX

Acetycholine, 19
Adrenaline, 6
Allergic persons, muffins for
  brown rice hazlenut muffins, 143
  buckwheat pumpkin spice muffins, 136
  maple pecan rye and millet muffins, 140
  millet raisin muffins, 134–35
  pumpernickel currant muffins, 141–42
  raw fruit muffins, 144
  rye, rice, and raisin muffins, 137
  steamed raisin muffins, 145
  tofu bran blueberry eggless muffins, 138–39
Allergies
  to chocolate, 133–34
  to corn, 132–33
  to cow's milk, 132
  to eggs, 133
  to wheat, 133
Almonds
  apricot almond jam, 159
  apricot almond muffins, 92–93
  cherry almond amaretto muffins, 89–90
  milk substitute, 132
  salmon rice almond muffins, 84–85
  tuna apple almond muffins, 80–81
  turkey cranberry almond muffins, 81–82
Amaretto
  cherry almond muffins, 89–90
  happy new year honey cake muffins,
    151–52
Ambrosia muffins, 49
Amino acids, 11–13, 88, 143
Apples
  no-egg bran apple muffins, 117–18
  pecan and apple bran muffins, 98–99
  tuna apple almond muffins, 80–81
Apricots
  almond and apricot muffins, 92–93
  almond apricot jam, 159
  pineapple and apricot minimuffins, 48
Arteriosclerosis, 14

Baking powder, 19–20, 132–33
Baking time, 24
Bananas
  carob banana boat muffins, 127–28
  cottage cheese banana topping, 161
  cranberry and banana nut muffins, 50
  hazelnut topping banana muffins, 100–101
  maple walnut and banana muffins, 90–91
  peanut butter banana delight topping, 161
  peanut butter banana muffins, 39
Beans
  black bean and rice muffins, 69
  carob bean, 17–18
  garbanzo bean sprouts, 33
  peachy beany spice muffins, 43
  pinto beans, 43, 115
  soybeans, 85
  spicy bean muffins, 115–16
Beta carotene, 52, 61, 62, 63, 153
Bioflavenoids, 19, 37
Black bean and rice muffins, 69
Blackstrap molasses, 8–9, 114
Bland, Jeffrey S., 28
Blintz muffins, 28
Blueberries
  buttermilk and blueberry muffins, 116–17

Blueberries (*continued*)
  sunflower blueberry muffins, 99–100
  tofu bran blueberry eggless muffins, 138–39
Bran, 11, 13–14, 29
  apple pecan bran muffins, 98–99
  no-egg bran apple muffins, 117–18
  tofu bran blueberry eggless muffins, 138–39
Breakfast ideal, 28
Breakfast muffins
  date and nut muffins, 35–36
  dynamite muffins, 30–31
  fig and nut muffins, 37–38
  hearty pear and pecan muffins, 36–37
  maple walnut muffins, 34
  peanut butter banana muffins, 39
  wheat germ raisin ginger muffins, 29–30
  wheat sprout muffins, 32
Broccoli mushroom cheese muffins, 73–74
Brunch muffins
  ambrosia muffins, 49
  coffee cake muffins, 45–46
  cranberry banana nut muffins, 50
  herbed minibiscuit muffins, 47
  orange marmalade poppy seed muffins,
    44–45
  peachy beany spice muffins, 43
  pineapple apricot minimuffins, 48
Buckwheat pumpkin spice muffins, 136
Butter, 17
Buttermilk, 20, 47
  blueberry buttermilk muffins, 116–17

Calcium, 9, 10–12, 14, 19, 35, 43, 47, 49, 54,
    59, 62, 70, 71, 73, 92, 93, 105, 114, 123,
    125, 144
Carbohydrates, 28
Carob powder, 17–18
  banana boat carob muffins, 127–28
  as chocolate substitute, 133–34
  mint and carob topping, 129
  mint carob cashew muffins, 128–29
  popcorn carob cheesecake muffins, 108–109
Carrots
  orange pecan and carrot muffins, 4, 55–56
  powerhouse carrot coconut muffins, 153–54

selection of, 52
Cashews
  carob mint cashew muffins, 128–29
  tofu cashew cheeseless cheesecake muffins,
    107–108
Cauliflower muffins, 54
Cheese
  blintz muffins, 71
  cheeseless cheesecake tofu muffins,
    107–108
  cottage cheese, 70, 71, 74, 161
  kasha mushroom cheese muffins, 74–75
  macaroni and cheese muffins, 70
  mozzarella, 72, 73
  mushroom broccoli cheese muffins, 73–74
  pizza muffins, 72
  topping, 126
  yogurt creamless cheese, 159
Cheesecake muffins
  cheeseless tofu muffins, 107–108
  heavenly cheesecake muffins, 111
  mocha kahlúa cheesecake muffins,
    124–25
Cherry almond amaretto muffins, 89–90
Chick pea sprouts, 33
Chives
  corny corn and chive muffisn, 77
  sour cream and chive muffins, 119–20
Chlorine, 50
Chocolate, 18
  allergy to, 133–34
  substitute for, 133–34
Cholesterol, 6, 11, 13, 14, 15–17, 18
Cholesterol reducing muffins
  blueberry buttermilk muffins, 116–17
  fruit 'n' nut oat bran muffins, 118–19
  no-egg bran apple muffins, 117–18
  sour cream and chive muffins, 119–20
  spicy bean muffins, 115–16
Choline, 85
Chromium, 9
Chutney (peach) and pumpkin muffins, 149,
    150
Cinnamon raisin whole wheat English
    muffins, 156

164

Coconut
  ambrosia muffins, 49
  orange parsnip snowballs, 59–60
  powerhouse carrot coconut muffins, 153–54
Coffee cake muffins, 45–46
Conserves, 25
Cooling, 24
Copper, 9
Corn
  allergy to, 132–33
  chive and corny corn muffins, 77
  herbed corn muffins, 65
  popcorn muffins, 108–109, 110, 112
  potato corn and sunflower muffins, 76
Cornmeal, 12–13
Corn oil, 15
Cortisone, 6
Cottage cheese, 70, 71, 74
  banana cottage cheese topping, 161
Cranberries
  banana nut and cranberry muffins, 50
  turkey cranberry almond muffins, 81–82
Currant pumpernickel muffins, 141–42

Date and nut muffins, 35–36
Diabetes, 14
Diet muffins. *See* Low-calorie muffins
Dynamite muffins, 30–31

Eggs, 71
  allergy to, 133
  substitutes for, 133
English muffins (cinnamon raisin), 156
Enzymes, 15, 44, 78
Exotic muffins
  happy new year honey cake muffins,
    151–52
  popovers, 155
  powerhouse carrot coconut muffins, 153–54
  pumpkin peach chutney muffins, 149, 150
  whole wheat cinnamon raisin English
    muffins, 156

Fats and oils, 15–17
Fatty acids, 88, 92, 141

Figs
  raisin, fig, and nut spread, 160
  nut and fig muffins, 37–38
Flax seed, 62
Flours, 9, 11–13
Food processors, 22
Freezing batter, 24
Freezing muffins, 42
Fruit. *See* specific fruits
Fruit and nut muffins
  apple pecan bran muffins, 98–99
  apricot almond muffins, 92–93
  banana maple walnut muffins, 90–91
  banana muffins with hazelnut topping,
    100–101
  blueberry sunflower muffins, 99–100
  cherry almond amaretto muffins, 89–90
  dynamite breakfast muffins, 30–31
  fuzzy navel peach muffins, 96–97
  oat bran fruioat bran fruit 'n' nut muffins,
    118–19
  papaya pumpkin seed muffins, 94–95
  plum and peanut muffins, 93–94
  prune and pistachio party muffins, 123–24
  raw fruit muffins, 144

Garbanzo bean sprouts, 33
Ginger raisin muffins, 29–30
Gluten, 9

Happy new year honey cake muffins, 151–52
Hazelnuts
  banana muffins with hazelnut topping,
    100–101
  brown rice hazelnut muffins, 143
  fig, raisin, and nut spread, 160
Heavenly cheesecake muffins, 111
Herbed minibiscuit muffins, 47
High-density lipoproteins, 16, 65, 114
Honey, 7–8
Honey cake muffins, 151–52
Hypoglycemia, 14

Icing. *See* Toppings
Insulin, 6

Iron, 9, 11, 14, 35, 43, 47, 50, 59, 62, 74, 92, 112, 116, 123, 125, 144, 151

Jack-ó-lantern muffins, 125–26

Kahlúa
   happy new year honey cake muffins, 151–52
   in maple tofu whip topping, 109
   mocha kahlúa cheesecake muffins, 124–25
Kasha mushroom cheese muffins, 74–75
Kugels
   bird's nest pineapple noodle muffins, 78
   zucchini kugel muffins, 105

Lecithin, 11, 18–19, 23, 45, 85, 114, 115, 116, 118, 119, 134
Lemon and squash muffins, 61
Lesser, Michael, 3
Linoleic acid, 14, 63
Low-calorie muffins
   cornmeal muffins, 112
   fifteen-calorie popcorn nosh, 110
   heavenly cheesecake muffins, 111
   peachy pecan muffins, 3, 106–107
   popcorn carob cheesecake muffins, 108–109
   tofu cashew cheeseless cheesecake muffins, 107–108
   zucchini kugel muffins, 105
Low-density lipoprotein, 15, 16, 18
Lysine, 11–13

Macaroni and cheese muffins, 70
Magnesium, 9, 10, 43, 47, 50, 114, 144
Maimonides, Moses, 3
Manganese, 50, 99, 116
Maple syrup, 8
   pecan maple rye and millet muffins, 140
   tofu maple whip topping, 109
   walnut and maple muffins, 34, 63–64, 90–91
Margarine, 17
Marmalade and poppy seed muffins, 44–45
Mattson, Fred, 16
Matzo meal muffins, 79

Maz EPA, 84
Meal muffins
   bird's nest pineapple noodle muffins, 78
   black bean and rice muffins, 69
   blintz muffins, 71
   corny corn and chive muffins, 77
   corny potato sunflower muffins, 76
   kasha mushroom cheese muffins, 74–75
   macaroni and cheese muffins, 70
   matzo meal muffins, 79
   mushroom broccoli cheese muffins, 73–74
   pizza muffins, 72
   salmon rice almond muffins, 84–85
   tuna apple almond muffins, 80–81
   tuna melt muffins, 82–83
   turkey cranberry almond muffins, 81–82
   vegetarian meal-in-a-muffin, 85–86
Methionine, 11
Metric conversion chart, viii
Milk
   sour milk, 20
   substitutes for, 132
Millet
   flour, 13
   maple pecan rye and millet muffins, 140
   raisin millet muffins, 134–35
Minimuffins
   ambrosia minimuffins, 49
   banana maple walnut muffins, 90–91
   cranberry banana nut muffins, 50
   fruit 'n' oat bran muffins, 118–19
   heavenly cheesecake muffins, 111
   herbed minibiscuit muffins, 47
   oat bran fruit 'n' nut muffins, 118–19
   pineapple apricot, 48
   popcorn carob cheesecake muffins, 108–109
   raw fruit muffins, 144
   tofu cashew cheeseless cheesecake muffins, 107–108
Mint carob cashew muffins, 128–29
Mixing ingredients, 22
Mocha kahlúa cheesecake muffins, 124–25
Molasses, 8–9, 114
Mono-unsaturated oils, 16–17
Muffin tins, 23

Mushrooms
  broccoli cheese and mushroom muffins,
    73–74
  kasha mushroom cheese muffins, 74–75

Niacin, 9, 35, 77, 137
Nuts, 88
  almonds, 80, 81, 84, 89, 92, 159
  cashews, 107–108, 128–29
  cranberry banana nut muffins, 50
  date and nut muffins, 35–36
  fig, raisin, and nut spread, 160
  fruit and nut muffins, 30–31, 88–101
  hazlenuts, 100–101, 143, 160
  peanuts, 16, 39, 93–94, 160, 161, 162
  pecans, 3, 36–37, 55, 56, 59, 98, 106–107,
    140
  pistachios, 123
  toasting of, 23–24
  walnuts, 34, 35–36, 37–38, 56, 59, 63, 90,
    151–52

Oat bran, 14, 29, 45, 65, 80, 114, 115, 116,
  118, 119
  fruit 'n' nut oat bran muffins, 118–19
Oats, 12
Oils and fats, 15–17
Olive oil, 16, 114, 115, 116, 119
Omega 3 fatty acids, 62, 141, 151
Omega 6 fatty acids, 141
Orange marmalade, 44–45, 96–97
Oranges
  ambrosia muffins, 49
  carrot orange pecan muffins, 4, 55–56
  marmalade and poppy seed muffins, 44–45
  parsnip and orange snowballs, 4, 59–60
  rind of, 19
Oven preheating, 23
Oversize muffins, 23

Pans, 23
Pantothenic acid, 2–3, 29, 74
Papaya pumpkin seed muffins, 94–95
Parsnip and orange snowballs, 4, 59–60
Party muffins

carob banana boat muffins, 127–28
carob mint cashew muffins, 128–29
happy new year honey cake muffins,
  151–52
jack-ó-lantern muffins, 125–26
mocah kahlúa cheesecake muffins, 124–25
prune and pistachio muffins, 123
Peaches
  bean and peach muffins, 43
  fuzzy navel peach muffins, 96–97
  pecan and peach muffins, 3, 106–107
  pumpkin peach chutney muffins, 149, 150
Peanuts
  banana and peanut butter muffins, 39
  banana peanut butter delight topping, 161
  fig, raisin, and nut spread, 160
  milk substitute, 132
  oil, 16
  plum and peanut muffins, 93–94
  yogurt peanut butter topping, 162
Pear and pecan muffins, 36–37
Pecans
  apple pecan bran muffins, 98–99
  carrot orange pecan muffins, 4, 55–56
  maple pecan rye and millet muffins, 140
  orange parsnip snowballs, 59–60
  peachy pecan muffins, 3, 106–107
  pear and pecan muffins, 36–37
  zucchini raisin and nut muffins, 4, 56–57
Pectin, 88, 98, 115, 118
Peppers
  selection of, 52
  yellow pepper muffins, 62–63
Phosphorus, 14, 35, 125
Pineapple
  ambrosia muffins, 49
  apricot and pineapple minimuffins, 48
  bird's nest pineapple noodle muffins,
    78
Pinto beans, 43, 115
  spicy bean muffins, 115–16
Pistachio and prune muffins, 123–24
Pizza muffins, 72
Plum and peanut muffins, 93–94
Polyunsaturated oils, 10, 15, 16

Popcorn, 12
  carob cheesecake popcorn muffins, 108–109
  fifteen-calorie popcorn nosh, 110
  light and fluffy cornmeal muffins, 112
Popovers, 155
Poppy seed and marmalade muffins, 44–45
Potassium, 9, 10–12, 35, 39, 49, 50, 54, 56, 59,
    62, 63, 73, 77, 93, 90, 92, 100, 116, 118,
    123, 125, 127
Potatoes
  corny potato sunflower muffins, 76
  potato muffins, 58–59
Powerhouse carrot coconut muffins, 153–54
Preparation
  mixing ingredients, 22
  oven preheating, 22
  plumping raisins, 23
  tins, 23
  toasting nuts, 23–24
Protein, 10, 11, 12, 13, 14, 28, 37, 43, 69, 70,
    71, 81, 82, 85, 88, 92, 93, 94, 107, 112,
    115, 123, 134, 143, 153
Prunes and pistachio muffins, 123–24
Pumpernickel currant muffins, 141–42
Pumpkin
  buckwheat pumpkin spice muffins, 136
  jack-ó-lantern muffins, 125–26
  peach chutney and pumpkin muffins, 149,
    150
Pumpkin seeds, 14
  papaya pumpkin seed muffins, 94–95

Raisins
  fig, raisin, and nut spread, 160
  ginger raisin muffins, 29–30
  millet raisin muffins, 134–35
  plumping of, 23
  rye, rice, and raisin muffins, 137
  steamed raisin muffins, 145
  whole wheat cinnamon raisin English
    muffins, 156
  zucchini raisin and nut muffins, 4, 56–57
Raw fruit muffins, 144
Reheating, 24–25
Riboflavin, 9

Rice
  black bean and rice muffins, 69
  hazlenut and brown rice muffins, 143
  rye, rice, and raisin muffins, 137
  salmon rice almond muffins, 84–85
  vegetarian meal-in-a-muffin, 85–86
Rice flour, 11
Rye flour
  maple pecan rye and millet muffins, 140
  rice, rye, and raisin muffins, 137
Rye sprouts, 3

Safflower oil, 15
Salmon rice almond muffins, 84–85
Seeds, 14–15
Selenium, 54, 70
Sesame seeds, 14–15
  milk substitute, 132
Sodium, 11, 12, 14, 11
Sour cream and chive muffins, 119–20
Sour milk, 20
Soy flour, 11
Special party muffins. See Party muffins
Sprouts, 32–33
Squash
  lemony squash muffins, 61
  selection of, 53
  zucchini. See Zucchini
Storage, 24, 25
Sugar, 6–7
  bad effects of, 6–7
  substitutes for refined sugar, 7–9
Sulfur, 50
Sunflower oil, 15
Sunflower seeds, 14
  blueberry sunflower muffins, 99–100
  corny potato sunflower muffins, 76
  toasting of, 23–24
Sweeteners
  conserves, 25
  frozen fruit juice concentrates, 7
  honey, 7–8
  maple syrup, 8
  molasses, 8–9
  sugar (refined), 6–7

168

Sweet potatoes
    maple walnut and sweet potato muffins,
      63–64
    selection of, 52–53

Thiamine, 6, 9
Tins, 23
Tofu
    bran blueberry eggless tofu muffins, 138–39
    cashew tofu cheeseless cheesecake muffins,
      107–108
    maple tofu whip topping, 109
    vegetarian meal-in-a-muffin, 85–86
Toppings
    apricot almond jam, 159
    banana cottage cheese topping, 161
    banana peanut butter delight, 161
    calories in, 158
    carob mint topping, 129
    cheese topping, 126
    fig, raisin, and nut spread, 160
    maple tofu whip topping, 109
    peanut butter yogurt topping, 162
    vanilla sauce, 160
    yogurt creamless cheese, 159
Triglycerides, 6
Triticale sprouts, 33
Tryptophan, 12, 13
Tuna
    apple tuna and almond muffins, 80–81
    tuna melt muffins, 82–83
Turkey cranberry almond muffins, 81–82

Vanilla sauce, 160
Vegetable muffins, 52–53
    broccoli cheese and mushroom muffins,
      73–74
    carrot orange pecan muffins, 4, 55–56
    cauliflower muffins, 54
    corn muffins, 76, 77
    herbed corn muffins, 65
    lemony squash muffins, 61
    parsnip orange snowballs, 4, 59–60
    potato corn and sunflower muffins, 76
    potato muffins, 58–59

    sweet potato maple walnut muffins, 63–64
    vegetarian meal-in-a-muffin, 85–86
    yellow pepper muffins, 62–63
    zucchini kugel muffins, 105
    zucchini raisin and nut muffins, 56–57
Vitamins
    A, 19, 35, 54, 55, 56, 62, 71, 73, 92, 93, 77,
      78, 96, 105, 116, 123, 125
    B, 1, 3, 6, 9, 10–13, 15, 29, 32, 37, 44, 54,
      58, 59, 62, 71, 73, 81, 88, 105, 123, 134
    C, 19, 32, 54, 58, 62, 73, 78, 96, 105, 116
    D, 71
    E, 3, 10, 15, 16, 71
    K, 71
    niacin, 11, 137
    pantothenic acid, 2–3, 29, 74
    thiamine, 6, 9

Walnuts
    banana maple walnut muffins, 90–91
    date and nut muffins, 35–36
    fig and nut muffins, 37–38
    fruit and nut muffins, 30–31
    happy new year honey cake muffins,
      151–52
    maple walnut muffins, 34, 63–64, 90–91
    orange parsnip snowballs, 4, 59–60
    sweet potato maple walnut muffins, 63–64
    in vegetarian meal-in-a-muffin, 85–86
    zucchini raisin and nut muffins, 4, 56–57
Wheat allergy, 133
Wheat bran. *See* Bran
Wheat flour, 9
    substitutes for, 133
Wheat germ, 9–11
    raisin ginger wheat germ muffins, 29–30
Wheat milk, 132
Wheat sprouts, 32–33
    muffins, 32
Whole wheat flour, 9

Yellow pepper muffins, 62–63
Yogurt, 20, 119–20
    creamless yogurt cheese, 159
    dill-yogurt sauce, 84

Yogurt *(continued)*
    peanut butter yogurt topping, 162

Zinc, 9, 14, 10, 44, 47, 94

Zucchini
    kugel muffins, 105
    raisin nut and zucchini muffins, 4, 56–57
    selection of, 53